IS HE DEAD?

This book is based upon a true story of rape, incest, child abuse, torture, spouse abuse, and murder. Written by the original homicide investigator, it is based on an after-the-fact police investigation into the lives of two innocent children, their mother and a not-so-loving stepfather.

© 2014 Rick H Drew
Written by Rick H Drew
Edited by Pauline Hamian and Iris Baker
Cover Design by Marcos Conde

The moon hovered above with cascading streaks of dull light through the canopy of cypress trees. The murky creek water trickled southward with a blanket of rotting leaves and moss. The large cypress trees towered like skyscrapers above the shallow creek bed. Closer to the water line, large, ghost-like cypress knots extended from the ground. Just as Tom shut off the motor, there was a loud splash in the water. A six or seven foot long alligator whipped his tail across the surface.

He ordered both Amanda and Melissa out of the truck. He pointed to a grassy area next to the water and demanded, "You stand right there and don't fucking move!"

"What about alligators?" Melissa cried. Tom opened a tool box that was mounted on the back bed of his truck and removed a large machete. "It's not going to matter in a few minutes," he said coldly as he removed a machete from its canvas cover and walked over to Amanda and Melissa.

DEDICATION

This book is dedicated to a young police officer and a dear friend of mine, Thomas Alan Bartholomew who was killed in the line of duty in Kissimmee, Florida during an act of heroism.

CHAPTER 1
Shots Fired, Man Down

The following is based on a true story; the names have been changed, as well as some of the details to protect the innocent.

This story rattled even the most case-hardened police officers as the evidence in this case began to unravel. The children in this case were able to survive for almost a decade under some of the most unpardonable conditions. Some of what they endured you may find difficult to believe, but these sorts of things do happen in our society as much as we hate admit it.

I worked for a medium-sized police department in the metropolitan Orlando area, a town known for its ranching, cowboys, and Disney World. And me, I was a narcotics investigator, and I was on call on the afternoon these events began to surface.

On call didn't officially begin for me until 5:00 p.m. I left the police station at 4:30 p.m. My work was done for the day so I decided to go home a little early. I stopped at a 7-11, and had just re-filled my Big Gulp cup.

Minutes from my home a radio tone alert sounded. It's a grisly sound, sort of like the sound a computer makes when it connects with the internet, but much louder and it really gets your attention. The dispatcher gave the call out to a patrol officer. My supervisor came over the radio and instructed me to respond. I unenthusiastically agreed and responded in my unmarked police car.

The call was dispatched as a subject down, possible gunshot victim. I got there a little after 5:00 p.m. The paramedics were loading a white male victim into the ambulance. The officer on the scene advised me that when she arrived she found him on the ground, bleeding and cursing. She went on to say it appeared he had run from an apartment and had collapsed a few feet from the street.

She explained that she had asked him what happened and he had replied,

"My son shot me."

I stepped up into the ambulance,

"What happened?" I asked.

He replied, "No questions."

I asked him again and his response was the same. So, I stepped out of the ambulance and shut the double doors as its crew was preparing to drive off. My supervisor just arrived and yelled out to me.

"Go with them, get in!"

"Damn it!" I thought, so much for going home early."

Being a narcotics agent I didn't want to be stuck with a shooting investigation, but I had no choice at that point. So I hopped up and in.

Riding in the back of an ambulance speeding down the street with its emergency lights and siren on is not the most comfortable place in the world to be. Ambulance drivers are much worse than police officers. They really drive crazy. But I tried to make the best of it. I asked him what his name was. He responded again, "No questions."

He yelled this time. So I asked him again what happened and who shot him. He blurted back at me words that, I guess if I was in his shoes, I may have used myself.

He said, "Fuck you, I will handle it."

"Hey buddy, that's not how we do things," I responded.

"I just want to know who shot you," I said, with all the compassion a discontented policeman could assemble.

He yelled back at me, "I'll take care of it myself!"

Even though he was being nasty to me I still felt sorry for this man. I didn't like to see people in this condition. From what I could gather, his son had shot him, but why? He started looking pretty bad. His face was losing color and his body began to convulse. My guess was he was about to die. He was gurgling and that usually means the end is pretty close. However, I needed to know who shot him. I knew the only way to attain a dying declaration was if the person giving it knew he was dying. So I said,

"Listen to me buddy, you're going to die. Do you understand that? I need to know who shot you."

Oh my God, at that very moment all hell broke loose. You would have thought I had shot the man. The paramedic let me have it with both barrels.

"Are you crazy? You can't say that to my patient!" she scolded..

I realize the paramedic's job is save lives and for me to tell the patient he was going to die was contrary to that objective, but that's the only way a dying declaration can work.

A couple of years back, the same paramedic and I responded to a pretty bad traffic accident. A young man riding a motorcycle had been hit by a semi-truck. She was talking to the victim and trying to stabilize him. She asked me to check his lower extremities. When I looked down at his feet, I discovered they were barely connected. Hell, I wasn't used to that. I exclaimed, "Oh my God!" A little too loud, I'm afraid.

The kid immediately went into shock. She ran me off then too, so I guess she held a grudge. The boy lived, but his feet were a mess.

When we arrived at the hospital the paramedics rushed him into the emergency room. I sat outside for moment then walked to the ambulance entrance.

The entrance was an automatic door that opened when a gurney rolled onto a pressure pad, but when I stood on the pressure pad it didn't open. I jumped up and down on it, to no avail.

"That figures," I thought. So I walked around to the patient entrance of the ER.

All the movies and TV shows in the world can't prepare you for the real drama in an emergency room. I watched as this man went into cardiac arrest. The ER team went to work. I stood back and looked on in amazement. He was a pretty big guy. My guess at the time was he was close to 200 pounds and in his mid-thirties. He must have been at least six feet tall. He had medium brown hair that just fell just below his ears. He looked like the kind of guy who just didn't want to let go of the seventies.

His body convulsed as the electricity charged through it. Hell, I even jumped when they did that. The doctor repeated the same ritual two more times. He was passing out orders like a Marine drill sergeant. I watched as he held up a huge hypodermic needle and stabbed it directly into the man's chest.

"Damn!" I said out loud.

If he had been conscious, that would have hurt like hell! The team's pace was slowing down and the doctor seemed to be running out of options. A few minutes later, he yelled, "Time?"

A nurse blurted out, "18:33".

Immediately the doctor replied, "Time of death: 18:33".

They all stepped back and began removing their surgical gloves and gowns. They just walked away and left him there with all the tubes and wires protruding from his body. I stood there for a minute just staring at him. There was blood on the floor, along with all sorts of medical waste and sterile bandage wrappers. No matter how you look at it, death just isn't pretty. The skin loses color almost immediately. The smell of death fills the room fast. It's a musty smell. I just don't think you can ever get used to it. I took a deep breath walked over to him and covered his body with a sheet.

I thought that was the least I could do.

CHAPTER 2

A Child's Tearful Confession

The emergency room receptionist walked up to me and said,

"He has family in the lobby, you know."

I walked out and saw a small-framed woman. She introduced herself to me as Melissa Jenkins. She said she was the victim's wife. Just looking at her, one might think she had lived a pretty rough life. Another lady sitting next to her introduced herself to me as Kelly St. Francis. She said she was Melissa's employer at a local restaurant. There was a third woman, a teenager with short brown hair and freckles. Her name was Amanda and she was the victim's daughter. They didn't know he was dead yet. I asked Melissa if she had a son. She replied, "Yeah, I have a son. His name is Robert. Why?"

"Do you think Robert could have shot his dad?" I asked.

Before she could answer, Amanda interrupted me and asked to speak with me privately. Her Mom sat quietly so I agreed and we walked outside. She was very uneasy and shaking like a leaf. "But who wouldn't be under the circumstances," I thought to myself. She wanted to know if he was dead. I said, "I don't know."

She asked again, "Is he dead?"

Well, of course I knew he was dead, but delivering death notices was not my favorite part of police work, and we were at the hospital, so I told her she needed to ask the doctor. She was persistent and said, "My God, he's going to kill us!"

I asked, "What do you mean? Amanda, is your brother involved in this?"

I watched her eyes swell and turn red as tears began rolling down her face. She just stared at me, she didn't say a word. Who knows what she was thinking at that moment? She took a big

5

breath and as she spoke her voice cracked. But her response was very clear,

"We've been abused and we stole a gun," She blurted.

My face dropped and I know my expression had to be one of pure shock. This time, I took a deep breath and said,

"Amanda, stop. Don't say anything further, not right now, not right this minute, okay?"

She stood there silently and seemed to be waiting for me to tell her to continue. A murder is a big case and it's best to consult with someone with more experience. I stepped aside called my lieutenant on the radio. I explained to him what had just taken place. I asked him to send a detective to the hospital as soon as possible and he replied,

"10-4, I have one there."

"That's a relief," I thought. And then I realized he was referring to me.

Amanda and I walked back inside just as the doctor was breaking the news to Melissa that her husband was dead.

"Something isn't right here," I thought.

The doctor had just informed her that her husband was dead and all she did was shake her head from side to side. No tears and no outburst of emotions. It wasn't normal. I hated delivering death messages because I just couldn't bear the aftermath. Some people, mostly women, fainted when they heard that a loved one had died. I would guess that in almost all cases of the messages I had delivered in the past, the recipient had at least cried.

The lieutenant arrived a few minutes later and together we advised Melissa Jenkins (Amanda's mother) that we needed to conduct an interview with her daughter. She didn't even ask why. She just agreed. I also told her I would be advising Amanda of her constitutional rights.

Amanda was transported first to her house to get her shoes, and then escorted to the police station. Mrs. St. Francis drove her Mother to the station.

Meanwhile, the SWAT team was scouring the area for the shooter. The details were not very clear at the time, but Robert Jenkins was a suspect. I was told he was only 14 years old and we didn't have any idea where he was.

It was after 9:00 p.m. when we finally settled down to conduct an intense interview. Just as I was about to get started the captain invited himself to participate. He was the kind of person that the average guy just didn't like. He was very intelligent and he let everyone know it. He used huge words to intimidate his listener. I guess it made him feel smarter. I didn't want him there, but I didn't complain. Hell, he was the boss.

Reading Amanda her rights was an emotional experience for everyone.

"You have the right to remain silent. Do you understand that?" I asked.

She responded with a very respectful, "Yes, sir."

I continued, "You have the right to an attorney before any questions. Do you understand that?"

Again she responded, "Yes sir."

When I had completed advising her of all her rights, I asked Amanda and her mother if they both understood their rights as I had explained them. They each replied they did, and agreed that Amanda would waive her constitutional rights.

I had Amanda sign a rights card acknowledging that she had been advised and waived. She agreed to provide me with a sworn taped statement.

"It started almost ten years ago," Amanda began.

"We was abused ever since Tom came into our lives." Amanda continued. She was fidgeting in her seat and breathing hard as she spoke. Her story was horrific and incredible. It sounded almost rehearsed. We talked for more than two and a half hours. I mostly listened. Having been in law enforcement for five years, I didn't think there was much left out there that could shock me. This young lady and her brother had conspired, planned and orchestrated an elaborate plot to kill the man they both called dad.

CHAPTER 3

Was it Murder or Self Defense?

I felt like a tremendous burden had been dumped on me. If her statement was true and this man had tortured her and brother, then I would somehow have to prove it to be true. Being a policeman isn't just about making an arrest, as so many people may believe; it's about uncovering and reporting the facts. After the interview I had to follow procedures.

"Amanda, you have to go to the juvenile detention center."

"Why? I just want to go home with my mom!" she cried.

She was becoming very emotional. She grabbed her mother and held on tight. I had to pull them apart and it wasn't easy for me. I think everyone in the room was crying at that point.

A patrolwoman responded and knocked on my office door. She didn't have a clue what we all had just gone through in the interview room. She walked in and told Amanda to stand up against the wall. She told her to spread her legs apart and proceeded to search her.

"Put your hands behind your back," the officer said to Amanda. The officer removed her handcuffs from her handcuff pouch and placed a cuff, first on Amanda's left hand, then on her right.

"Mom!" Amanda cried.

Finally, there was an outbreak of emotions from her mother. Melissa sobbed loudly as the officer walked Amanda out of the room.

Meanwhile, the SWAT team was still turning the west side of town upside-down looking for Robert Jenkins, Amanda's little brother. The K-9 unit was out searching with their dogs, but somehow this little boy had managed to slip through the dragnet.

The next morning I had to appear in juvenile court to testify on behalf of the state at a hearing before the judge of the Circuit

Court. The press had blanketed the courthouse lawn scouring for information on this high-profile murder. The fact that two children had turned against and killed a parent caught the attention of Good Morning America and other TV programs nationwide.

After the judge was seated, the Clerk called the case.

"Do you have money to hire an attorney?" The judge asked Melissa Jenkins.

Melissa was shaking and answered the question with a simple,

"No sir."

The judge ordered a public defender and declared her insolvent. Insolvent meant she was broke and could not afford to hire an attorney. After a short wait a public defender entered the court room. Her name was Maria Alvarez and she and I had a history. Up until that point she and I had been like two positive ends of a magnet, we just couldn't come together. I investigated and arrested drug dealers and she defended them. Maria read over the arrest affidavit and the judge asked the prosecutor Larry Vaughn if he was prepared.

"Yes, Sir, Judge," he answered.

He explained the basics of the case, at least what he knew of at that time. Then he put me on the stand. First you have to go through the motions.

"Do you swear to tell the truth and nothing but the truth?" The clerk asked me.

I responded, "I do."

After providing a brief explanation of the case, the judge ruled there was probable cause to detain Amanda for homicide. He then ordered her retained at the detention center. I stood up and asked the judge if I could again be heard. He permitted me to speak and I asked if he would release Amanda to her mother.

"Detective, are you sure about that? This is a serious crime we are talking about here," he said.

"I know, Your Honor, but I don't think this child would be a danger to anyone else at this point."

The judge asked the state attorney and public defender if they concurred with my recommendation. The state attorney did not agree, but the judge went along with me, so Amanda was released to her mother. The next day the press reported that the investigator assigned to the case made a request of the court to release the homicide suspect. The Chief of Police called me to his office and gave me a verbal thrashing.

"What the heck were you thinking?" he asked me.

"Chief, that child has already lived through enough horror. I don't think she needs any more from us," I replied.

"You had better hope she behaves, Detective. From now on, keep your opinions to yourself," the chief warned me sternly.

Later on in the afternoon, we received a call from a lady by the name of Patricia Langly. She advised the dispatcher that Robert was in her home. A patrolman and a detective responded to her mobile home and transported Robert to the police station. When they brought him into my office he was obviously frightened to death, but was relieved to hear his stepfather was dead. Robert went through the same process as his sister. His mother sat with him while I advised him of his rights. Like his sister, he waived his rights and provided me with a sworn statement. It was like listening to a tape-recorded conversation of Amanda's statement. One thing that struck me as highly unusual was Robert's choice of words for the male and female genitalia. When he described certain acts perpetrated by his stepfather, he referred to the vagina as "cunt" and to the penis as "dick." These were words I never thought a kid would use in the presence of his mother.

Once the interview was completed, Robert was processed through the juvenile system, and then released to his mother.

The next day the lieutenant decided I would remain as the primary investigator on the case. He assigned Detective John Singleton to assist me. The allegations of child abuse, incest and rape had to be thoroughly investigated. Most of the alleged abuse occurred in Tennessee. The Chief decided to send Detective

Singleton to Tennessee to conduct an in-depth background investigation.

Detective Singleton spent two weeks in Tennessee uncovering facts that would turn most people's stomachs. His investigation made up two volumes over four inches thick each. We spent a month putting this puzzle of horror, child abuse, incest, theft, fraud, rape, and eventually murder together. This book is the result of numerous interviews, record searches, police reports, and statements made by friends, co-workers, babysitters, and family members. It took our team well over a month to assemble this puzzle spanning nearly ten years of these children's lives. I was really split on how to tell this story. Some folks recommended I hire a ghostwriter, but I felt passionate about writing it in my own words. However, I am a cop, not a writer, so the story you are about to read is simple, plain and to the point.

CHAPTER 4

Where it all Started (October 1974)

The story began in 1974, on a cool autumn morning in the hills of Tennessee. The beauty could only be appreciated if you were there to witness it for yourself. The trees were dancing in the wind and displayed the vibrant colors of autumn on almost every leaf. Almost everywhere in Tennessee is beautiful, but this place is alive with color and tradition, and a wedding was about to take place.

Charles Thomas Jenkins and Melissa Jones were getting married. It was October of 1974. Amanda Jones was only eight years old and Robert Jones, her little brother was six.

At the time, Melissa Jenkins was a little more than 5' 2" tall and, soaking wet, she weighed maybe 100 lbs. She had a zest for life and embraced every day as she awakened to face it. She was pretty when she dressed up and even prettier when she put a little make up on. She was married once before for a short time. Her two children; Amanda and Robert, were from her first husband, Bill Jones.

Tom was a burly fellow, a little under six feet tall and every bit of 185 pounds. He had brown hair parted on the right side and cut just above the bottom of his ears.

Amanda was a tiny little thing. She had curly brown hair and big brown eyes. She loved to play with her dolls and playing house. She also enjoyed helping her mom with her little brother. If there was one person she loved more than anything else in the world, it was her little brother Robert. Some folks back then described Amanda and Robert as being two peas in a pod.

Robert was two years younger than Amanda, not a big boy, kind of small for his size, but he was all boy. It was nothing for Robert to come in out of the yard covered with a fresh coat of top soil. Sometimes the only thing white on Robert was his eyes. They shared the same bedroom, one half with old Tonka trucks and little green army men, the other half with Barbie dolls and Barbie clothes spread out meticulously on the floor.

    Tom and Melissa bought a mobile home and had it parked in a trailer court. The court wasn't very big and all the trailers were parked very close to each other. When the person in the trailer next to you sneezed, you would hear it.

CHAPTER 5

Adoption Celebration

On November 19, 1974 Tom and Melissa Jenkins filed a petition for adoption at the County Court House. In the petition, Tom said he had grown to love both Amanda and Robert as his own children since his marriage to Melissa, which was only one month earlier.

That night Tom and Melissa decided to celebrate the pending adoption.

"Let's go celebrate and have some drinks," Tom said to Melissa.

Tom got dressed in a white long-sleeved shirt with the shirt tail partially tucked in. He put on black pants with button-down pockets. It was obvious that dressing up was not something Tom did routinely. People like Tom buy a suit when they need one – whatever kind is popular at the time. The next time they need a suit may be ten years later. They just keep wearing the same suit, and never realize it is no longer in style.

Melissa wore a white blouse with ruffles on the front with a pair of red stretch-slacks and a pair of white open-toe high heels. They left the house acting like two teenagers.

"Bring us a couple of margaritas grande," Tom said in his southern twang. "Make 'em real strong," he added.

After three drinks, Tom turned to Melissa and said. "Damn, I'm feeling good, let's go for it tonight."

He reached under Melissa's blouse and ran his index finger up and down her stomach. He stopped at her navel and began caressing it with slow in and out motions. Melissa was getting excited. Tom told her to follow him. He grabbed her hand and led her to the men's room. When he got to the door he pulled Melissa in and said, "Come on."

Melissa replied, "I can't go in there."

"Come on, Baby," Tom said.

He pulled her into the restroom and they began to kiss passionately. Tom pulled down Melissa pants and sat her up on the counter. He lowered his pants and they began having sex in the men's room. They were making quite a bit of noise, causing a teenage busboy to walk in and investigate.

"Get the hell out of here!" Tom yelled.

The kid turned and walked out without uttering a word. This sexual encounter lasted no more than a few minutes. When they were finished Melissa told Tom that she had to pee.

Tom said, "Pee here," pointing to a urinal. Melissa still hadn't put her pants back on. She stood in front of a urinal and made a lame attempt to do what she was told. An older patron walked in and saw her standing there with no pants on, straddling the urinal. Tom looked at him and asked, "What the hell is your problem?"

"Nothing buddy, I don't want no trouble," the elderly man said.

The man walked up to the second urinal and stood there. Melissa finished peeing, mostly on the floor. Tom and Melissa put their pants back on and returned to their table. Tom ordered one more drink but Melissa had had all she could handle. She was getting anxious to go home and tugged on Tom's arm. Tom looked over at her and asked, "What? I ain't ready to go yet."

"We need to get home to the kids, Tom." Melissa whispered.

Tom turned to Melissa and, without any notice, drew back a closed fist and struck her right across the jaw, knocking her clean out of the chair she was sitting in. The chair broke apart when it hit the floor. Melissa fell back hitting her head against the wall. She started crying and screamed, 'Why Tom? Why?" Realizing what he had done, Tom reached down and lifted her up.

"Come on let's go home," he said.

Chapter 6
Don't Ever Say a Word

After returning from the bar, Tom gave Melissa a couple a painkillers and put her to bed. Robert and Amanda were both sleeping. Tom walked into their bedroom and stood over Amanda. Her body was covered exposing only her face. He pulled the sheets down and lifted her gown away from her chest. He stared at her tiny breast. She moved and he stepped back. He was touching her forehead while she slept. He backed up and started stroking himself. The movement and noise woke Amanda. As her eyes opened she felt Tom touching her. Tom saw she was awake and stepped back covering himself with his hand. Then he said to Amanda,

"You better not ever say a word to anyone about this, or I will kill you and your little brother. Do you understand me?"

He grabbed her by the neck and repeated in a whisper, "Do you hear me? It's not so bad, baby," he whispered, as he forced her to perform oral sex on him. "You'll learn, baby."

Tears were running down her face as her body trembled in fear. When Tom climaxed, he threatened Amanda as he walked out, "Don't forget, Amanda, not a word, or you know what will happen. You know I will do it, don't ya?"

The next morning; Amanda was up early watching cartoons. Tom walked into the living room and said cheerfully, "Good morning," but Amanda didn't reply.

Tom grabbed her by the face, looking directly into her eyes.

"I said good morning, you got a problem?"

Amanda pulled her face away and Tom took off his belt and struck Amanda across her back, leaving a nasty red welt. Amanda screamed out in pain. Tom struck her more than a dozen times after that. When he stopped swinging the belt, Amanda fell on to the floor. Her back and legs were numb and Tom walked away saying, "Don't you ever jerk away from me".

"You just remember what I told you last night," he said as he shut the door on his way out of the trailer.

Amanda stayed on the floor crying. Robert walked in the room crying also after seeing what had just happened to his sister. He put his arms around Amanda and said, "It's okay, Amanda."

CHAPTER 7

Robert Left his Tonka Toys on the Floor

Tom had been working all day at the lumber yard and was covered in a blanket of pine sap. It wasn't unusual for Tom and his co-workers to take Kerosene showers. It was the only thing that would cut all the pine tar from their hair and skin. He got out of his pickup truck with a beer in one hand and a gas can in the other.

When he opened the trailer door, it slammed against the wall so hard that the doodad shelves Melissa had on the walls rattled violently. The door sprung back and hit his hand, knocking the bottle of Budweiser beer he was drinking on to the floor. Beer spewed everywhere.

"Son of a bitch!" he yelled.

"Damn it that was my last fucking beer!"

"Hi honey!" Melissa said cheerfully and then the phone rang.

Melissa picked it up. "Hi Momma," she said, placing the phone to her ear.

"Momma, you know that ain't true. He loves these young'uns like they're his own." she said almost whispering.

"What the fuck is she saying?" he said again, but much louder this time. "What the fuck is she saying? Your fucking mother makes me sick and she better stay the fuck out of our business," exclaimed Tom. Next time we go over there she bess just keep her fucking mouth shut or I'll shut it for her", Tom yelled, as he sat down on the plastic covered sofa removing his boots.

"She means well, Tom. Don't be so hard on Momma, she just wants what's bess for these kids," Melissa said.

Tom mumbled, "She ain't got the sense God blessed a billygoat with," he grunted, then stood up and walked towards the bathroom.

"Damn it!" Tom yelled as he stepped on one of Robert's Tonka toys.

"Robert, I've told you a thousand times to put your fucking toys away! Why in the hell don't you do what you're told?" Tom screamed.

"Come here, son!" Tom called, as he removed his belt.

"Come here, damn it!"

"Bend over!" he yelled.

Tom swung the belt as if he was hitting an adult. The belt hit with such velocity that it crackled like thunder when it struck Robert's behind. Robert jumped and bounced around trying to break free from Tom.

"It's going to be worse if you run away from me, Robert!" Tom screamed.

Tom swung again, this time hitting Robert on his back. Robert was crying hysterically, trying desperately to break the hold Tom had on his arm.

"Pull away from me, will ya?" Tom screamed, as he struck Robert again and again.

"Now, what did I tell you to do, Robert?" Tom asked.

Robert was crying and gasping for breath, unable to respond to Tom fast enough.

"That's too fucking slow" Tom screamed.

He hit him again, this time just below his neck. Robert was barely conscious when Tom stopped swinging.

"Stop it Tom, damn it, stop it!" screamed Melissa. "You are going to kill him!"

Tom grabbed Melissa by her hair and said, "I know what the fuck I am doing. Your son don't never listen and I'm teaching him a fucking lesson," Tom whispered in Melissa's ear. "You don't whoop these kids, so I have to do it for you."

Amanda ran into the living room and bent down over Robert. "Get off that boy, Amanda!" Tom yelled.

"Get the fuck off!" he repeated.

Amanda was crying as she covered Robert's limp little body. Tom grabbed Amanda by the shoulder and said, "I told you to get up!" He slapped her on the back of her head, knocking her on to the floor.

Amanda jumped up and ran to her room. Later that evening, Tom picked up Robert and carried him into the bedroom. As he was placing Robert in the bed, he woke up.

"Hey sport, you know you were wrong, don't you son? I don't like having to whip you, boy. Hell, it hurts me worse than it does you. When I tell you to put away your toys, I mean put them away," Tom whispered to Robert, as he tucked the sheets over his chest.

"Yes, sir," Robert replied, whimpering from the lingering pain of his beating.

CHAPTER 8

The Sitter Discovers Abuse

The next day, Tom dropped the kids off at the babysitter on his way to work. Maria Walker had been the kids' sitter for a few months.

"All right, Maria," he said to the babysitter, as he left. And to the kids, he yelled, "I'll see you guys this afternoon after work."

Robert and Amanda were sitting at the kitchen table in Maria's house having a snack.

"Robert, be careful with that milk, son," Maria said.

Before the words could leave her mouth, Robert spilled the entire glass on his shirt and pants. Maria stood up and walked over to Robert to clean him up. When she reached towards him he pulled away.

"What's the matter, son?" she asked.

"I am not going to hit you. It was just an accident. We'll get you all cleaned up. We'll just wash those clothes and you can take a bath," she said, as she lifted him from the chair.

Robert winced in pain when she touched him.

"What's wrong, son?" she asked.

"Nothing," Robert replied.

"Let me get these clothes off you then," she said to Robert.

"No, I don't want to take a bath," cried Robert.

She lifted up his shirt,

"Oh my God!" she thought to herself.

Robert had welts and red stripes all over his back, neck, and shoulders.

"This is terrible," she thought out loud.

"You can't say nothing, Mrs. Walker! He'll whip me again!" Robert said. "I don't want another whipping okay?" Robert begged.

"Come here Amanda; let me see your back," Maria said.

When she uncovered Amanda's back she saw old stripes and scars on her back as well. The first thing she thought about was the movie Roots, when the black slaves were beaten by the slave owners leaving similar marks on their skin.

Maria picked up the phone and dialed Melissa's mother at work.

"Ruth," she said, "I need you to come over here and take a look at these kids. They both look like they've been beaten half to death!"

Ruth dropped by later that afternoon.

"Take a look at this!" she said, as she lifted Robert's shirt.

"Oh my God," Ruth cried out. "I don't understand how Melissa can let that man do this to these kids. I'm going to talk to her and Tom for that matter," Ruth declared, as she walked out the front door.

"Thanks, thanks for calling me, Maria," Ruth called out as she left.

CHAPTER 9

Grandmother Takes a Stand

"It's been six weeks since we've been to Momma's house," Melissa said. "Why can't we just go over there for a just little while?"

"Let them come over here if they want to see you so bad," Tom replied.

"OK, fine," Melissa said as she picked up the phone to call her mother.

A few hours later there was a "knock, knock" on the screen door.

"Melissa, yoo-hoo," Ruth called to her. Ruth and her husband Chuck then entered the front door. Ruth was Melissa's mother. She was getting old, but she still had some spunk in her. Her thin legs were covered in varicose veins and she hadn't shaved under her arms in years. At one time, she had reddish-brown hair, but now it was mostly grey and thinning.

"Tom, I was over at Mary Walker's house today. God Almighty, son! What are you doing to these children?" she yelled. "They both got welts and scars on their backs! Tom, you need to stop being so rough on these young'uns." Ruth yelled.

Tom screamed back, "You mind your own fucking business!" How I discipline these young'uns is my damn business, you stupid bitch!"

Ruth's voice grew stronger as she yelled back,

"Don't you cuss at me like that, Tom Jenkins. It just ain't right," Ruth grabbed her husband's hand and said, "Let's go Chuck. Let's get outta here right now."

Melissa's dad was still getting around pretty good but not like he used to. His head was balding and what hair he had left was gray. He had lost quite a bit of weight with his age, but for the most part he was healthy.

"Ya'll ain't going nowhere. Sit down", Tom ordered.

Tom walked up behind Chuck and pushed him. Chuck lost his balance, slamming face first on to the floor. His fall was somewhat broken by an old boot being used to prop open the door. His nose hit first and as he collided with the heel of the boot, blood spurted everywhere

"You damn bastard, Tom Jenkins. He's an old man. Why the hell do you have to do the shit you do. Why don't you pick on somebody your own size?" Ruth screamed.

"Awe shit, Ruth. I didn't mean to hurt him."

"You're just a damn coward!" Ruth screamed.

Tom turned beet-red when she said that. He grabbed Ruth by her wrist and as she tried to pull away, Tom just squeezed harder.

"Who in the hell are you calling a damn coward?" Tom yelled.

Chuck reached up and grabbed Tom's leg and Tom just slung him loose. Tom squeezed Ruth's wrist harder and twisted. Ruth was straining to break free and Tom released his grip. Ruth fell over the coffee table. Every word out of her mouth at that point was a curse word.

"You damn child abuser!" she screamed.

Immediately the room became silent. Ruth braced herself on the coffee table trying to stand up. She had one hand on the floor and one on the table, Tom walked over to her and stomped on her arm. Everybody in the room could hear it when it happened. It sounded like a tree branch breaking. He broke her wrist, snapped it clean into two. The bone was now protruding through her skin. She yelped like an old coon dog.

"You son of a bitch!"

"Fuck you, fuck both of you. Get the fuck out of my house," Tom said as opened a bottle of beer.

At the hospital the doctor had to perform surgery for three hours on Ruth's wrist to straighten it. Chuck's lip required two stitches.

"I just can't figure him out," Chuck said, as he helped Ruth into the car.

"He's dangerous, Ruth. He's going to kill somebody, he is. You just watch and see, Ruth".

"He scares me, honey. He scares me real bad," Chuck whispered.

"I'm real worried for those two kids," Ruth said.

The next morning, Tom drove over to Mrs. Walker's house. He got out of his truck and slammed the door. Mrs. Walker heard him drive in and walked out on her porch.

"Morning," she said as Tom walked up to her porch.

Tom replied, "Fuck your good morning!"

He opened her screen door and let himself in. "What in the world do you think you're doing, Tom Jenkins?" Mrs. Walker shouted,

Tom stood directly in front of her and said, "Let me tell you one thing. Keep your fucking nose out of my business! You got something to say about how I raise those kids, you be woman enough to call me, you hear? Next time you run your mouth, lady, I'll put those bruises on your ass, you understand me?" he yelled.

Mrs. Walker stood right in front of Tom and said, "There's too many police in this town for you to think you can get away with something like that, Tom Jenkins!"

"Well, you just fucking try me, okay? Maybe I'll put a hurting on that crippled fucking husband of yours!"

Mrs. Walker's husband had severe epilepsy.

"You better just leave my house right now before I call the police!" Mrs. Walker screamed.

Tom stepped out of the porch and slammed the screen door. Just before closing his truck door, Mrs. Walker yelled,

"Tom, you touch my husband and I'll kill you myself!"

Tom looked up at her, shook his head and closed his door.

CHAPTER 10
Over the Line

Late one evening, Tom settled down in his brown faded Lazy Boy recliner. He looked over at Melissa.

"Put Amanda and Robert to bed."

Melissa grabbed Robert by his little hand and said, "Come on, little one. It's time to hit the sack."

Wearing his Incredible Hulk pajamas, he pulled away but quickly lost in the tug of war with his mom.

"You won't like me when I'm mad," he said, as he flexed his little muscles acting like the Incredible Hulk. Amanda was sitting on the living room floor brushing the hair on one of her Barbie dolls. She was wearing a light pink ankle-length nightgown with little Barbie Doll prints all over it. Amanda stood up and walked to the bathroom. She took out her toothbrush from the medicine cabinet and brushed and flossed her teeth.

Amanda and Robert shared the same bed. Robert jumped on to the bed and started bouncing. Amanda grabbed him by the arm and pulled him down on to his knees.

"Are you crazy? Don't do that Robert, you'll get a beating," she said.

"I'm the Incredible Hulk, nobody can hurt me," giggled Robert.

Amanda put her finger to his lips and said, "Shh ……"

They both got on their knees next to the bed as Amanda said their prayers. Minutes later they were both sound asleep.

The trailer they lived in was kind of small but it served its purpose. Everyone had a place to sleep and eat. The walls were decorated with black velvet paintings. Tom's favorite painting was a nude female on black velvet. He had an Elvis painting behind the sofa. Melissa had the walls cluttered with shelves and all sorts of knick-knacks. The walls were light-colored wood paneling, the norm for trailers and mobile homes at that time.

Melissa was reading the National Enquirer on the sofa and drinking a 16-oz Royal Crown Cola, not daring to say a word about what just happened to her mother. She was terrified of Tom and didn't want to receive the same treatment. She lay there reading until she dozed off.

Tom looked over at her and saw she was sleeping.

"Hey, you asleep?" he asked.

She heard him but decided not to answer. Tom walked into the bathroom dropping his pine sap stained clothing on the floor. Lifting up his right arm he pulled away a large sticky glob of pine tar from his skin.

"Damn, that hurt," he muttered.

He turned on the shower making it as hot as he could stand it and stepped into the bath tub. Shortly after closing the shower curtain he heard a knock at the door. It was Amanda,

"I need to pee pee," she said.

"Come on in, Amanda. I got the curtain pulled-to," he said quietly.

As soon as Amanda came in she lifted up her nightgown and pulled down her panties to her ankles. Tom drew back the curtain and looked on as she sat on the toilet. He could feel himself getting excited and took a bar of soap and lathered his body. He began stroking himself as he looked on. Amanda reached for the toilet paper and Tom spread the curtain a little more so he could see her.

Amanda stood up and pulled up her nightgown to her neck holding it to her chest with her chin. She removed a wad of toilet paper from the roll and cleaned herself. When she finished, she tossed the paper into a trash can on her way out. She pulled up her panties and quietly shut the door, leaving Tom to his shower. Tom stepped out on to the floor and grabbed a towel to dry his hands. His reached down into the trash and removed the tissue from the container. He placed it under his nostrils and took a slow, deep breath to inhale the aroma from Amanda's used toilet paper. He was stroking himself as he inhaled the paper. In only seconds he climaxed, just thinking about having sex with his 8-year-old stepdaughter. He stepped back into the shower and finished washing.

Amanda had seen him watching her

He wrapped a towel around his waist, walked into the living room and woke up Melissa.

"Let's go to bed," he said.

"I'm tired."

CHAPTER 11
Runny Eggs

Melissa was fixing a pot of grits, bacon and eggs for breakfast. The house was full of the delicious odor of cooked bacon. Amanda and Robert ran into the kitchen and sat down at the table. Melissa asked,

"How ya'll sleep last night?"

"Oh, perty good," replied Robert.

Amanda said she was hungry so Melissa fixed both their plates and poured them a glass of cold milk.

Tom walked into the kitchen dressed for work. His clothes smelled like pine trees and his old boots, well, that was a different story. Melissa asked Tom what he wanted for breakfast.

"Hell, I don't know. Just fix me up something."

Tom sat down and Melissa put grits and two eggs cooked over-easy on his plate.

"You know, I really have grown to love these two kids."

"I don't think it's right that I'm raising them for that worthless piece-of-shit father of theirs who ain't doing nutt'n'."

"I love them you know," Tom said, as he slurped down some hot, black coffee.

A sense of peace ran down Melissa's spine. She thought that had to be the nicest thing she had ever heard him say. Tom used his fork to cut into an egg bursting the yolk.

"Damn it, Missy! How many fucking times do I have to tell you I don't like my eggs running all over my God damned plate? You want to give me salmonella?" Tom yelled as he slung the plate into the wall. Eggs and grits splattered all over the floor.

The egg yolks slowly crept down the wall. He pushed the table as he stood up, knocking Robert from his chair. Robert screamed, "Amanda!"

Amanda jumped up from the table and ran to her bedroom. Melissa was on the floor helping Robert up when she muttered,

"Don't ever hurt my young'uns again, Tom Jenkins".

"What the fuck did you just say?" Tom yelled.

He grabbed Melissa by the hair and lifted her to her feet. He took his free hand and slapped her in the face. As he struck her, her lip exploded, splattering blood on to Tom's shirt. Her teeth looked like she had coated them with red lipstick. Melissa swung a fist at Tom but missed. He grabbed her around the neck and began choking her. As she gasped for air, her face and lips turned blue. She lost consciousness and slipped out of Tom's hands on to the floor. Tom walked out, slamming the door behind him. Both Amanda and Robert huddled over their mom, crying as she lay on the floor grasping for breath and weeping hysterically.

CHAPTER 12
Left Alone at Home (September 1976)

It was Friday afternoon and both kids were excited that it was Friday and the bus was late dropping Robert and Amanda off. It was Labor Day weekend and they had no school for two days. They got off the bus and walked over to a gas station in front of the trailer park. Amanda had two dollars and bought two RC Colas and two Moon Pies. They ate and drank as they walked home.

"Why is mom's car here?" Robert asked.

"I don't know, maybe she's home early today," Amanda replied.

The trailer door was unlocked. Amanda and Robert walked in and both yelled out, "Mom!" at the same time.

Robert walked into the kitchen and saw a note on the dining room table.

The note read,

Dear Robert and Amanda,

Me and Dad have gone to the mountains for the night. I will call you and give the phone number when we get there. Dad made sandwiches and put them in the refrigerator. Stay in the house, we will be back tomorrow afternoon

Mom and Dad.

P.S. Amanda, you are in charge

"Oh shit!" Amanda said as she read the letter. "They're not home and they ain't coming home tonight. We are by ourselves."

Amanda opened the refrigerator looking for the food.

"There ain't no sandwiches in here!" she yelled.

She opened the pantry and saw there was no bread or peanut butter.

"Damn, we ain't got no bread and no peanut butter either!" Amanda said.

"I think we got to cook something."

She opened the freezer and had a choice of frozen chicken breast or hamburger meat. Amanda asked Robert which he preferred. Robert said hamburgers.

"We ain't got no bread or buns," Amanda told him.

Robert told her that he had some money in his piggy bank and that his Mom had money in her night table drawer. The two of them searched through the house and managed to locate two dollars and thirty six cents.

"Okay, you go to the store and I will thaw out the hamburger meat," Amanda said.

Amanda took out 5 lbs of hamburger meat and put it in the sink. She turned on the water and put the meat underneath it. Robert was yelling for her to go with him. Amanda yelled back,

"All right!"

The two of them left the trailer and took off running towards the store.

Amanda left the water running on the hamburger meat, but she didn't remove the stopper from the drain. The sink overflowed and the water ran down the cabinet on to the floor. As the kitchen floor flooded, the water began seeping first into the living room carpet, and then underneath the front door on to the metal stairs leading up to the trailer.

Amanda and Robert arrived at the store and realized the buns only cost 79¢. They checked out and decided to play pinball with the remaining change.

"We don't need to hurry, it's going to take a while for the hamburger to thaw." Amanda said.

Amanda handed Robert three quarters and took three for herself. They played pinball for twenty or thirty minutes and then left the store.

"It's not bad being alone," Robert stated.

They walked to the trailer playing catch with the hamburger buns.

When they arrived at the trailer, it was dark. "What's that noise?" Amanda asked as they approached the front door.

"Oh shit! Oh my God!" Amanda screamed.

Robert yelled, "What the …?"

They saw the water pouring out from under the front door. Robert opened the door and water gushed out on to his shoes. Amanda ran in and turned the water off.

"We're dead, we're fucking dead!" Amanda screamed.

The kitchen floor was covered with water and a paper bag filled with garbage had broken apart and garbage on the kitchen floor, garbage was strewn all over the kitchen floor.

Robert ran towards the back of the house to get towels from the bathroom and quickly discovered the carpet was soaking wet.

"Amanda, the carpet is soaked too. It's real wet, what are we going to do?" he asked.

Amanda told Robert to get the mop and all the towels, "We have to get this cleaned up before Mom and Tom get home tomorrow!" she said.

They worked on cleaning up the water and garbage until 11:00 p.m. and managed to dry the kitchen floor, but weren't so lucky with the carpet.

"We are still dead, you know! As soon as Dad walks on the carpet he will know!" Amanda screamed.

"Shit, let's eat," said Robert

Amanda took the hamburger meat and made four patties. She threw the rest in the garbage. Robert put a large frying pan on the gas stove and turned it on.

"You want to use butter or lard?" Robert asked Amanda. "Use butter," Amanda replied.

At 12:00 a.m. they sat at the kitchen table and filled their bellies with hamburgers.

"That was just about the best hamburger I ever had," Robert told Amanda.

"It was good, wasn't it?" Amanda replied.

They washed up the frying pan and dishes and went into the living room to watch television. They put towels on the floor under their feet and fell asleep watching a re-run of Kung Fu.

They woke up at 11:00 a.m. when Melissa walked in the front door. Melissa told them good morning and commented on how clean the kitchen was.

"Mom you didn't leave us any sandwiches - we had to cook," Amanda said.

Tom came in and walked through the living room and immediately noticed the wet carpet.

"What the hell is this?" he asked. Amanda told him that the sink had overflowed and the water went everywhere.

He turned and said, "Melissa, I told you they would fuck it up. You can't trust these two idiots with anything."

Melissa looked at Tom and said "Why didn't you fix their sandwiches yesterday?"

Tom laughed and said, "There wasn't enough bread to make sandwiches for us and them too."

Melissa yelled very loudly at him, "How could you do that?"

Tom didn't say a word. He walked back in the bedroom and changed clothes. When we came back into the living room he was wearing socks and lost his temper when his feet got wet.

36

"You know, neither one of you are going to amount to a damn thing when you grow up. You're too fucking stupid," he said in an irritated voice.

Melissa sat down at the kitchen table and Tom walked up behind her and kicked the dining room chair out from underneath her. Melissa fell on to the floor and cried out,

"What the hell was that for?" Tom looked down at her on the floor and said, "Don't you ever raise your fucking voice at me in front of these young'uns! Now, you call somebody to come dry this damn floor up," Tom said as he walked back across the carpet.

CHAPTER 13

Tom Shoots up a Gas Station

It was December, 1976. It was going to be the family's third Christmas since Tom and Melissa were married. Amanda and Robert were both very excited. Amanda had recently celebrated her 10th birthday and Robert's 8th birthday was fast approaching. Both were sitting on the floor in the living room looking through the Sears catalog. Amanda was using a green felt tip pen to mark all the toys they wanted for Christmas. First on her list was Miss Piggy, second was Barbie with extra-long blonde hair with matching ear rings and necklace. She put two circles around the Bionic woman action figure. When Robert saw a toy he liked, he would point to it and Amanda would circle his choices for him. What he really wanted wasn't in the catalog. Robert wanted a mini bike.

"All I want is a mini bike, nothing else," Robert said to his sister.

"I want the one down at the hardware store," he said, "The red one".

Tom walked into the living room,

"Mom and me are going to the club tonight," he said.

Robert responded, "I want to go! I want to go!"

Tom told him he had to stay home with his sister. Robert started crying and demanded to go. Tom yelled over Robert's crying,

"Shut up Robert, you're not going!"

Melissa came out of the bathroom wearing a white knee-length dress and high heels. She was wearing coffee-colored lipstick with just a touch of blush on her cheeks.

"How do I look?" she asked, as she twirled around in a big circle.

"You look good enough to eat, baby," Tom replied. "Let's go," Tom said. "Lock the door behind us Amanda, and don't stay up past 10 o'clock, you hear?"

Tom and Melissa stayed at the club until it closed and both sat and drank beyond their limits.

"Okay, folks we're closed. I am sorry but we gotta lock up," the bartender shouted.

Tom and Melissa walked outside, both of them stumbling. "You want me to drive, Tom?" Melissa blurted out.

"I'll fucking drive," Tom mumbled.

He pulled on the door and as it opened he fell back on to the ground.

"Damn, I'm drunk," he said, laughing.

They had about four miles to drive home. The only thing between the bar and their trailer was a service station. Tom drove past the service station going a little over eighty miles an hour.

"Shit, we're out of fucking gas," Tom yelled.

He recklessly turned the steering wheel without slowing down the car. The tires screamed and smoke billowed from the wheel wells as Melissa slammed up against the passenger door and window. "Damn it, Tom! What the hell you doing? You trying to kill me or something?" she hollered.

"We're out of gas," he replied.

"The Delta station is closed," Melissa said, as they pulled up to the gas pumps.

Tom honked his horn over and over. Melissa was begging him to stop.

"Come on, Tom. Let's go. We can get gas tomorrow, honey," she pleaded.

Tom rolled down his window, "I know you're fucking in there, Paul. Get out here. I need some damn gasoline!" he yelled.

Paul was the owner of the gas station. The lights came on and a voice came back."I'm closed Tom! Come back tomorrow!"

Tom's face turned red as beet, as it usually did when was he was angry. He took an old chrome-plated 38-caliber revolver from underneath the seat. Melissa screamed, "No, Tom, don't do this. Tom, please."

"You're fucking closed, huh? I'll show you closed!" Tom said as he stepped out of the car, falling back on the door still feeling the effects of his margaritas. He pointed the gun at the front door of the station and yelled, "You got one minute to turn on this fucking pump!" Tom was holding the gun with the barrel facing the ground. He tripped and fell and as his right hand hit the ground the gun went off. It sounded like a cannon going off. Melissa screamed out for him to stop. Tom stood up and pointed the gun at the front window of the station and ripped off five more rounds into the store. Glass windows were shattering with every explosion from the gun's barrel.

Paul screamed out, "Are you fucking crazy, I'm calling the cops, Tom! Damn it, I got kids in here!" he yelled.

"Turn on the damn gas pumps, Paul," Tom replied.

"All right, all right!" Paul replied angrily. "What pump you want on?"

"Ethel," Tom replied.

CHAPTER 14
Off to Jail

It was just turning day break and there was a loud banging on the front door of the trailer.

"What the hell!" Tom yelled. "Who is it?" Tom yelled again. There was still no answer, but the banging on the door continued.

"Damn it!" Tom yelled as he put on his pants. As he walked to the door he screamed, "Somebody is getting a fucking ass whooping right now!"

When he opened the door three Athens police officers were standing there. Tom tried to slam the door on them, but one of officers grabbed his arm and pulled him outside of the door. Tom resisted by swinging his fist at the officers and cursing. He hit one of the policemen in the face. A third policeman tackled Tom knocking him to the ground. They pinned him face first in the dirt and managed to handcuff him. The officers had to drag Tom to the patrol car. One officer opened the door and the other two were attempting to put him in the back seat. Tom refused to get in. He put his legs out and began thrusting his knees and feet.

Melissa ran outside clad only in her house coat screaming and crying. She was so upset that mucus was running from her nose and mixing with the tears on her face.

"That's police abuse!" she screamed. "They beat my husband!" Melissa cried. She grabbed an officer, attempting to free his grip on Tom. The officer pushed her back and she launched a barrage of profanities and vulgar comments at him.

"Ma'am, if you don't stand back, you're going to jail too!" The officer screamed. Tom kicked one of the officers in the stomach as they tried to place him into the back seat. The policeman removed his night stick and slugged Tom on the back of the head. Tom dropped and actually went limp long enough for them to hog tie him. The senior officer read Tom his rights and then informed him that he was being arrested for discharging a firearm into the Delta gas station.

"You're fucking crazy!" Tom said, as he continued cursing and screaming obscenities at the officers. Tom was booked into the county jail on a felony charge. Later on that afternoon he was released on bail.

Nobody knew exactly why, but the charges against Tom were suddenly dropped. It's not certain, but it is rumored that Tom made a visit to Paul at the gas station and somehow convinced him to change his mind about prosecution.

After hearing the charges were dropped, Tom was talking to Melissa in their bedroom, "There ain't no fucking cop or anybody else going to keep me to jail. I got too much fucking power in this county!" Amanda and Robert were listening through the door and tiptoed away to their bedroom.

"I told you," Robert said to Amanda.

"We can't never tell nobody." He said. "You're right, Robert," Amanda whispered.

"We can't never trust the police or anybody else," she said.

CHAPTER 15

Don't Spy on Us

After partying one Friday evening, Tom and Melissa came home drunk. Melissa opened the door to the trailer, and then Tom slammed it. The sudden noise woke up Amanda. Tom pulled Melissa close to him and said,

"Let's screw. Right here right now", he said. Tom unbuttoned Melissa's dress from the back and dropped it on to the floor. He unhooked her bra and threw it on to the sofa. His hands ran down her back until he reached her panties. He pulled down and lowered her panties to her knees and stopped. He pulled off his own shirt and stepped out of his pants. He was ready for action. Melissa got on to her knees and began performing oral sex. Tom pushed her on to the floor and mounted her. Melissa yelped out loud and they laughed it off. Tom stopped and poured them both a glass of Jack Daniels. In minutes, they were back on the floor making love like there was no tomorrow. Unbeknownst to either of them, Amanda had been standing in the hallway watching them. Tom caught a glimpse of her standing in the shadow. He stopped and yelled, "Damn it. Come here Amanda. You wanna watch, get the fuck over here!" Amanda hesitated, but Tom demanded she come into the living room. Amanda walked in and Tom made her sit next to her mother on the floor.

"Now, you just sit there," he said.

"This ain't right, Tom", Melissa said.

"She needs to learn not to spy on people," Tom told Melissa. Tom spread Melissa's legs and re-mounted her.

"Now you watch this," he said to Amanda as he began thrusting himself into Melissa. Tom couldn't take his eyes off of Amanda. Melissa began moaning. In some insane way she was beginning to enjoy this as Amanda looked on. "Come here!" Tom said to Amanda.

"Take off your nightgown and panties," he said.

43

"No!" Amanda replied, but Tom demanded she comply. She slowly removed her nightgown and exposed her tiny breast.

"Lay on your back, baby," Tom whispered. Amanda laid down on her back. Her entire body was shaking almost to the point of convulsions. Tom straddled her and lifted her up at the waist and removed her Blonde Barbie Doll panties. Tom pried open Amanda's legs and said, "Relax Amanda. Relax your legs. This ain't going to hurt or nothing."

"That hurts!" Amanda yelled.

Melissa, still intoxicated, finished up her Jack Daniels and muttered with a slight drunken slur, "Just relax honey, he isn't going to hurt ya."

Tom looked up and said, "It's too dry. She needs some lubrication."

He grabbed Melissa by her hair and told her to perform oral sex on Amanda. Tom watched from inches away. Melissa did just as she was told. She performed oral sex on her own daughter. Tom pushed Melissa off of Amanda. He positioned his body so he was lying on top of Amanda, but not putting any weight on her. Melissa guided Tom's into Amanda's. Amanda yelled out in pain.

"Relax honey, Just relax your muscles," Melissa whispered.

Tom penetrated Amanda but stopped after Melissa complained that Amanda was bleeding. He withdrew and masturbated. Immediately after he climaxed, he ordered Melissa to stop and get cleaned up.

"This is not right!" Tom yelled out to Melissa.

He told Amanda to go back to bed. Amanda was embarrassed, ashamed, and in pain but happy he reacted in the fashion that he did, instead of hitting or beating her for spying on them.

CHAPTER 16
Robert Killed a Squirrel

Christmas came and past and Robert was upset that Santa Claus forgot about his mini bike, but the things that Santa did bring were okay. What he liked the most was his Crossman single shot BB gun. It was early spring and Robert was hunting in the woods next to his house. He was stalking a squirrel who was now perched between two large limbs on an old pecan tree. The squirrel was eating on a walnut, poised for a perfect shot. Robert rested his elbow on a tree stump and took careful aim.

"Okay, I need to breathe normally and squeeze the trigger," Robert thought to himself. The BB was released with a gush of compressed air and the squirrel fell from the limb. He was kicking and convulsing when Robert got up to him. Robert raised the BB gun above his head and, with the butt of his rifle; he delivered a skull crushing blow to the squirrel's head. The squirrel's head was flattened into the ground. Robert picked it up by the tail and walked away feeling very proud of his first kill.

"Look what I got me!" Robert said as he walked into the house.

"One shot and he was dead," Robert shouted.

"What are you going to do with it?" Amanda asked him.

"Cook it," Robert replied laughing. "But first I have to skin it."

In the back yard behind the trailer, Robert took out his pocket knife and made a crude cut along the squirrel's belly.

"Oh my God!"

Robert's stomach churned as the squirrel's little heart became exposed. It was still pumping. Robert could feel his stomach twisting inside and out, so he leaned over an old stainless steel sink and let it go. He threw up until he had nothing left in his stomach. He couldn't even look at the squirrel again. He went inside and found a used shopping bag underneath the kitchen sink.

As he crept back up on the squirrel he closed his eyes and covered him up with the brown paper sack.

"I am sorry, little squirrel, for killing you," he said, as his eyes began to swell.

"I need a box," he thought. He scooped the squirrel up with the paper sack and lifted it up.

"Amanda, I need a box!" he yelled as he walked into their trailer home. Amanda went into her mom's closet and emptied a shoe box.

"Put him in here," she said.

"You do it," Robert replied.

Standing over a small hole that Robert and Amanda had just dug, Robert placed the box into the ground. Amanda shoveled dirt on top.

"Dear God, please take care of this squirrel and tell him when he gets to heaven that I am very sorry for shooting him with my BB gun,"

Robert prayed.

"I won't ever do it again, I promise," he concluded. "Amen."

CHAPTER 17

Don't Play in the House

Late one evening Amanda and Robert were running up and down the hallway sliding on their socks.

"Watch me!" Robert said as he ran down the hallway. He slid into the coffee table knocking over a framed photograph of his mother. Tom was sitting in the living room and yelled, "That's enough, don't play in the house!"

Robert walked slowly back to the end of the hallway and took off running towards the living room for one last slide. This time he tripped over a torn piece of linoleum and fell right into a knick knack table. Several shot glasses Melissa had collected fell to the floor and broke.

"Damn it!" Tom yelled out. Robert ran into his bedroom and slid underneath the bed. Tom followed him into the bedroom, reached under the bed and pulled Robert out by his arm.

"You stupid little shit!" Tom yelled as he dragged him back into the living room.

"Look what you did now, Robert. I told you to stop it, didn't I?"

"Go get the fucking broom!" Robert was already crying hysterically.

"Shut up!" Tom yelled. Robert just wailed louder. His mom was at work and he feared the worst.

"I tell you what. Put the fucking broom up, you little sissy. Use your hands," he said. Robert slowly began to pick up all the large broken pieces, leaving small slivers of glass on the floor.

"I can't get these without a broom," Robert whimpered. "Use your hand!" Tom said.

"I can't!" Robert screamed out. Tom grabbed Robert's hands and used them as if they were broom. Robert screamed in pain as a sliver of glass entered into his palm.

47

"Does that hurt?" Tom yelled.

"If you did what you're told, this wouldn't happen!" Tom yelled. Tom pushed his hand again on the floor without removing the sliver. Blood was creeping from the wound. Robert screamed out as another piece of glass cut into his thumb. Tom grabbed Robert by his face and said, "Next time I tell you something, you'd better do it!" Amanda ran into the closet and hid, covering herself up with dirty clothes. Every time Robert screamed she shuddered, trying to muffle the sounds of her brother's pain as she covered her ears with a pillow.

"What did you learn, Robert? Now, go wash your damn hands," Tom said. Robert ran into the bathroom and turned on the hot water. He pulled a piece of glass out of his thumb and cried out in pain.

Melissa came in from work right at 5:30 p.m. Robert was still in the bathroom crying, and Amanda was sleeping under the dirty clothes.

"What happened to you?" Melissa asked Robert.

"Nothing, Mom, I just got a piece of glass in my hand," he said. Melissa took his hand and put it under the light.

"There is still a piece in there," she said. Melissa told Robert to sit still. She took a sewing needle from her sewing kit and poured alcohol on it. She took Robert's hand and used the needle to dig out the piece of broken glass. She removed the glass and poured some alcohol on the tiny wound.

Melissa asked, "How did you do this?" Robert knew if he told his mother and she brought it up to Tom that Tom would just beat his mother, so he replied, "Mom, I accidentally broke one of your shot glasses and I got that glass splinter in my hand trying to clean it up.

CHAPTER 18

A Painfully Bad Report Card

Amanda was twelve years old and in sixth grade. She was attending Riceville Elementary School. She had just received her report card and she was scared to death to go home.

"Robert, I can't show Tom this report card. What do you think I should do?"

"I don't know, maybe change the F to a D or something."

"I can't do that, Tom is too smart. Then he would really beat me," Amanda said.

When Amanda and Robert arrived home Melissa was already there.

"Mom, I got a problem, a serious problem," said Amanda

"What's that, honey? What's wrong with you?" Melissa asked.

"Mom, I got an F in spelling on my report card. What am I going to do? Dad will kill me!"

"Tom's not going to kill you, honey," said Melissa. "He might whip you good, but you'll live."

"Robert, I think I am going to run away and get as far away from here as I can get," said Amanda.

"Where are you thinking of going?"

"I don't know but it's not right how he beats me and you. It's just not right."

Tom came home late that night after having an argument with Gene Cawthorn downtown. Tom opened the trailer door and he didn't say anything to anyone. He was wearing a small ball-type cap to cover his hair from pine tar. He had tar and sap all over his left arm. Melissa hollered, "Hey, honey," I'm in the bathroom." She was sitting on the toilet when Tom barged into the bathroom.

"What the hell crawled up you and died?" Tom asked Melissa.

"That ain't very nice," Melissa said. "Hell, I eat the same things you do."

"Amanda, Robert, come here!" he yelled. Amanda and Robert both entered the bathroom. Robert was holding his nose with his fingers to avoid having to smell anything.

"Amanda, what does it smell like in here?" Tom asked. Amanda and Robert started laughing.

"It smells like poop," Robert said.

"Poop hell," Tom replied.

"It smells like some'un done crawled up inside your Momma and died," Tom yelled laughingly. Robert and Amanda starting laughing with him, and even Melissa began to laugh.

Tom then ordered the kids out of the bathroom. He reached into the sink and turned on the hot water and grabbed a bar of lava soap. He was scrubbing his hands when Melissa told him.

"Tom, Amanda got herself an F on her report card." Tom looked up at her for a moment and looked back down at his hands.

"Let me see it!" Tom demanded.

"Shit, she got good grades except this one fucking subject."

"I been after her to study Tom, it ain't my fault!" Melissa said.

"Amanda, get your ass in here, girl," Tom yelled out. Amanda ran into the living room and responded with, "Yes sir?"

"Amanda, why do you have an F on your report card?" Tom asked. Her response was typical for a kid,

"I don't know"

"Have you been doing your homework?" Amanda looked like an old Mexican Hairless dog, standing there shaking.

"What are you going to do Tom?" Amanda asked. Tom looked around the room and then pulled off his belt.

"I am going to have to whip you, Amanda," he said. "Now go on into your room and take your clothes off and wait for me."

"I don't understand why you didn't know about this before it happened," Tom said to Melissa.

"I swear I didn't know Tom. She was hiding it from me, us, I mean. I didn't do nothing wrong, Tom. It was her!"

Tom walked into Amanda's room holding a leather belt. It was close to two and half inches wide. Amanda was hunched down in the far corner of the bedroom crying. Tom ordered her to get up and come to him.

"Take those panties off too," Tom told her. Amanda slipped her panties off and Tom told her to bend over and grab her ankles. Amanda bent down but couldn't quite reach her ankles. Tom stared at her backside for a moment, and then drew back his belt. When that belt hit Amanda, it sounded like lightning striking the house. Amanda screamed out in pain and straightened up her body. She tried to break free from Tom by jumping up and down and tugging on his grip. He maintained his grip and swung again, this time striking Amanda just below her shoulder blades. The skin began to welt after the blow. Amanda screamed again and pulled harder to break free of Tom.

"You know, fighting me is just going to make it worse," Tom yelled. He drew back the belt and again swung it towards her bottom. The belt made a painfully loud crackling noise each time Tom struck her. Amanda pulled away and Tom dropped the belt. He picked it up and swung it before getting a good grip. The belt buckle slammed up against Amanda's lower back. The impact broke the skin and Amanda shrieked in pain. The final torturous swing barely made contact, but the edge of the belt caught Amanda on her right thigh. Tom stopped swinging and said.

"The next time you get an F, it's going to be much worse. Now, put your clothes back on," Tom said.

Amanda was extremely shaken. She went into the bathroom and locked the door. She backed up to the mirror and saw red stripes and swollen ridges extending from side to side on her back. The welts were the same size as Tom's belt. Her back was still bleeding. When Amanda opened the medicine cabinet, she saw a razor. She took the razor out of the cabinet and sat down on the floor. She placed the razor against her wrist and had it not been for the thought of her brother Robert being left with Tom, she may very well have taken her own life. She stayed on the floor for a long time. Amanda stood up and placed the razor back into the cabinet. She removed a bottle of hydrogen peroxide and poured it over her shoulder over her wounds.

CHAPTER 19

Amanda's Teacher Suspects Child Abuse

One week later Amanda was at school in PE class and a teacher noticed a bruise on her leg.

"Mr. Bridges (Mr. Bridges was the principal of Riceville Elementary School), I think you need to speak with Amanda Jenkins. She has some pretty bad bruises on her - could be child abuse," the PE teacher told him. The principal had just recently received a call from a neighbor of the Jenkins' reporting the children were frequently left alone.

"I'd better notify the officials about this." he thought.

"This is Principal Bridges over at Riceville Elementary. I need to report a possible abuse situation," he said, speaking to someone on the telephone.

"We'll get someone over there right away," the official on the other end of the phone promised.

Within the hour, an investigator from Human Services arrived. She walked into the main office and asked to see the principal. "How are you doing?" the investigator said.

"My name is Mrs. Stringer and I am here to investigate the child abuse complaint."

Mr. Bridges led her to his office where Amanda Jenkins was waiting. Amanda stood up when up when they walked in.

"Sit down, honey," Mrs. Stringer told Amanda. "I just need to ask you a few questions about some things, okay?"

Amanda nodded and said she didn't mind talking to her.

"Amanda, now I want you to be honest with me, alrighty?" Mrs. Stringer said. "Amanda, I am an investigator for Human Services and I am here to help you."

"Tell me, is it true that you and your brother are left alone quite a bit when your mom and stepdad go out drinking?"

"No, Ma'am!" Amanda replied. "My parents do go out sometimes, but they always take me and Robert with them."

Mrs. Stringer asked her again, and she repeated her answer.

"Amanda, have you had a bad spanking recently?" The investigator asked.

"Yes, ma'am, I did get a right bad whipping not too long back."

"Can I see the mark on your back Amanda?" she asked.

Amanda obliged and lifted up the back of her shirt. Mrs. Stringer looked over her back and made a note in her notepad that Amanda had a two and half inch mark on her back consistent with being struck by a belt.

"Mrs. Stringer, you have to promise me you won't tell anyone about this! Promise me, I deserved the spanking cause I got an F on my report card!" Amanda cried.

"I am sorry Amanda but I will have to speak with your mother and stepfather," she told her.

"When?" Amanda asked. Mrs. Stringer explained to Amanda that she would have to drop by her home later on that day.

When school was out, Amanda met with Robert and told him what had happened with Mrs. Stringer.

"You can't go home, Amanda. You can't never go home again".

"I know it, but I don't know where to go. We got us a real problem here," she said.

"Let me think a minute," Amanda said. "Let's just get on the bus and we can figure something out."

CHAPTER 20
Amanda Runs Away

Amanda sat on the bus next to a girlfriend of hers named Donna Renard.

"What do you think he will do to you when he finds out?" Donna asked.

"I ain't sure, but I know it won't be too perty," Amanda told Donna.

"I figure he might just kill me tonight!" Amanda said, crying on the school bus. Donna told Amanda that both she and Robert could come to her house first.

"My Mom can help you. She's real smart about things like this," Donna said.

The bus stopped on Layman Road and as Donna, Amanda, and Robert were getting off, the bus driver stuck out his arm across the aisle and stopped Robert.

"Where do you think you're going, son?" he asked.

"We got permission to get off here," Amanda jumped in. The bus driver told her he wasn't aware of any permission, but he allowed the two to get off with Donna.

At the same time, Mrs. Stringer left the school and drove to the Jenkins' trailer. When she arrived, Tom and Melissa were home, but Amanda and Robert were not. They hadn't arrived home from the bus. The neighbors were going to door-to-door assisting Melissa and Tom looking for the kids.

Mrs. Stringer explained why she was there. Tom became extremely upset.

"No fucking wonder they didn't come home," he said.

"This is your fault. Who the hell do you think you are interfering in our business?" Tom accused Mrs. Stringer.

"Melissa, why don't you call the bus driver and see if he saw them this afternoon?" said Tom. Melissa tried for some time, but the phone just rang and rang. When the driver finally picked up the phone, he told Melissa both Amanda and Robert had been on the bus and they got off at the Renard house on Layman Road.

Melissa and Tom told Mrs. Stringer they wanted to continue but had to go get the kids. Mrs. Stringer asked if she could wait.

"Sure, fine with me," Tom said. "We'll be right back."

Meanwhile, Donna, Amanda, and Robert were just arriving at Donna's house.

"Momma, I got Amanda and Robert Jenkins with me. Can they come in?" Donna asked. Her mother Mrs. Reynard responded with a friendly, "Yes honey, of course they can." Mrs. Renard asked Amanda what she was doing on this side of town.

"My God, Amanda, what is wrong with you, honey? You're shaking like a darn leaf, child!" Robert was standing next to Amanda and he, too, was very upset.

"Are you sick?"

"No, ma'am. We just can't go home, no more. Me and Robert have to run away, or we may be killed."

"Child, there ain't nobody going to kill you two for crying out loud. What kind of story you telling me? Where do you plan on going, Amanda?"

"We don't care. Maybe a ditch or something! We just can't go home." Amanda replied.

Amanda was crying and trying to talk at the same time.

"Mrs. Renard, my stepdad does things to me. He goes all the way with me," Amanda said.

What do you mean, Amanda? Do you mean he has sex with you?"

"Yes, ma'am and with my brother, too!" Amanda exclaimed.

Mrs. Renard sat down in a rocking chair quietly for moment lost in thought,

"What can I do? My God this is awful!"

Amanda looked at her with a very sad face and said, "Ma'am, one time not too long ago, he got mad at me and my brother 'cause we was making noise in the trailer. He took out a BB gun and put it to my brother's head. Then, he put it up against my face, right against my eye. He told me if I didn't get out of the trailer right that minute he was going to shoot out my eye and then shoot my little brother in the head. We're real scared, I know it sounds crazy and wild and all, but it's true."

"What does your mother do about this, Amanda?" Mrs. Renard asked.

Robert jumped in, "If our mom tries to stop him, he just beats her, too."

"He really beats ..." Robert was interrupted by a violent knock at the door. Mrs. Renard opened the door and there stood Melissa Jenkins.

"Howdy, Mrs. Renard. Are my young 'uns over here?"

When Amanda and Robert heard their mother at the door, Amanda grabbed their coats and book bags and both ran back into Mrs. Renard's bedroom.

"Get over here, Robert." Amanda said, pulling Robert down behind the bed. Mrs. Renard didn't know quite what to do, so she just nodded and said.

"Yes, they're here. Come on in."

Tom was sitting in the car waiting. He turned on some country music during the ride home and everyone was quiet. When they arrived Mrs. Stringer was sitting in the living room. Tom said to Amanda.

"You know this lady, Amanda?"

"Yes," replied Amanda

"Do you know why she is here?"

"I think so," Amanda replied.

Tom asked Amanda in a fatherly manner, "Honey, why didn't you come home from school? You know there ain't nutt'n we can't work out."

Amanda nodded and said, "I know Dad. I'm sorry for running away like I did."

Mrs. Stringer asked about the whipping and Melissa answered, "We did have to whip her, but she doesn't usually get that bad a spanking. The problem was she brought home an F in spelling on her report card. Robert can tell you he ain't had no spanking lately, 'cause he ain't done nutt'n to warrant one."

When Mrs. Stringer asked about leaving the kids alone, Melissa again responded defensively.

"That's not true. Amanda did you tell this lady that? "

Mrs. Stringer told Melissa and Tom she needed to request a physical examination for Amanda and she would like to have her sit with a psychologist. Tom agreed to the physical but said he would not agree to a shrink.

"Okay," Mrs. Stringer said. I will make an appointment for her to see our doctor."

Tom said he could not agree to that, "We have our own doctor."

"All right, I guess that's okay," Mrs. Stringer replied. "Just make sure they send me the results, okay?"

CHAPTER 21

Child Services Begins an Investigation
(February 1978)

The next morning, Mrs. Renard called the Health and Human Services Department to report what had happened the night before. Mrs. Stringer was dispatched to her residence.

"Listen, I hate to get involved in things like this, but those children are in a great deal of danger," Mrs. Renard exclaimed. Mrs. Renard explained to Mrs. Stringer exactly what Amanda had told her regarding sexual and physical abuse. Mrs. Stringer thanked her for calling and assured her she had done the right thing.

Mrs. Stringer returned to Riceville Elementary school only to be told that both Amanda and Robert had been withdrawn and transferred to Westside Elementary School. When asked why they were switched, the principal Mr. Bridges said all he was told was that the kids were moving in with their grandmother.

Mrs. Stringer called Mr. Fletcher, the principal at Westside, and verified Amanda and Robert had been transferred. He said they were just enrolled that morning. Mrs. Stringer requested the school to follow-up on Mrs. Renard's report. She had Amanda respond to the principal's office.

"Amanda, how are you doing today?" Mrs. Stringer asked.

"Good," Amanda answered.

"Listen, Amanda. I need to know if your stepfather has ever sexually molested you."

"What?" Amanda exclaimed, acting very shocked.

"What are you talking about? No! Never! My stepdad is a great man and he is good to me and Robert."

"Amanda, do you remember what you told Mrs. Renard?" Mrs. Stringer asked. Amanda responded by denying everything Mrs. Renard had told the investigator.

"Now, why would Mrs. Renard lie to me Amanda?"

"I don't know, but it's not true!" Amanda replied.

"Amanda, why did you and Robert move to this school?"

"My mom and dad sold the trailer and we moved in with my grandmother," Amanda answered

Mrs. Stringer asked to see Robert while she was there. "Robert, have you ever been beaten or sexually molested by your stepfather?" Mrs. Stringer asked. Robert's response was one of shock. He told her that Tom was a great stepfather and he had always treated him and Amanda very well.

Three days later, Mrs. Mona Jones and her daughter Anne Jones drove down to Health and Human Services. They asked to see Mrs. Stringer. They were told she was out of the office, but she would return within the hour. Mona and her daughter Anne sat in the lobby and waited.

"Mrs. Jones, I'm Mrs. Stringer how can I help you?"

"Hi, this is my daughter Anne and we gotta talk to you about Tom Jenkins and what he's done to these children, my daughter included," Mona said. "We just want you to know that the situation at the Jenkins house is bad, it's real bad. We have been neighbors of theirs for quite some time."

"Do you know if they sold their trailer and moved out?" asked Mrs. Stringer.

"No I don't think so."

"Do you know if their trailer is for sale?"

"My uncle manages the trailer park where we live in and he hasn't told me anything about it. As far as I know they are still living there. Why do you ask?"

"No reason," Mrs. Stringer responded. "So why have the two of you come here today?"

"Anne here has told me some very disturbing things about Amanda, Robert and their parents. I have been meaning to call you for some time, but now I have to tell someone and get some help for those two kids. "Mr. Jenkins has sexually molested Amanda almost every weekend for the past three years. She said sometimes Mr. Jenkins takes Amanda into the bedroom and leaves Melissa and Robert in the living room. He has sex with that child!" She stopped to catch her breath before continuing.

"The boy is forced to have sick oral sex with that man and his mother, Mrs. Stringer!"

Mona went on to explain that Amanda and Robert are routinely left alone for extended periods of time, sometimes for an entire weekend. Then she added that Amanda had confided in her daughter that Tom puts that stuff in me."

"My God, what the hell does that mean?" Mona exclaimed. "Not too long ago, Robert accidentally broke a dang lamp. His mother whipped him, but Tom didn't think it was enough punishment, so he whipped that poor child again."

"You know what? I don't think those two are really married either." She added as if she suddenly remembered.

"Why do you think Amanda would deny all these allegations?" asked Mrs. Stringer.

"Hell, that's easy, she's frightened to death. She's afraid Mr. Jenkins will kill her and her brother."

Mrs. Stringer told Mona Jones and Anne that she didn't think Amanda would tell the truth if she had that much fear...

To this Anne responded thoughtfully, "You know, me and Amanda are good friends, and she told me all that stuff and I believe her. If you want her to be honest with you I think you might need me with you when you ask her again."

The next day Mrs. Stringer, Mona and Anne drove together to Westside School. Amanda was called to the office and when she walked in, Anne was not present. Mrs. Stringer asked her again if she had experienced any sexual or physical abuse at home. Amanda looked directly into her eyes and denied everything. Mrs. Stringer asked Mona and Anne to come into the office. When Amanda saw Anne her facial expression changed from defiant denial to that of a frightened child and she began to cry.

"It's true!" Amanda said bursting into tears. Mrs. Stringer handed her a napkin to wipe her tears. Amanda was unable to speak, she was crying so hard and whimpering, barely able to catch her breath.

"My God," Amanda said. "My God. He has been having sex with me for more than three years. He even forces us all to have sex together."

"What do you mean by that?" Mrs. Stringer said softly.

Amanda started crying again. "My mother is afraid of him. He will kill her and Robert, too, if we talk. He has told me a hundred times if I talk to anyone like you that he will kill me and my little brother." She attempted to gain her composure.

CHAPTER 22

A Botched Medical Examination (March 1978)

Mrs. Stringer explained to Amanda she would have to make an appointment for her to have a medical examination. Amanda became frantic, declaring she did not want to see a doctor.

It was explained the exam was mandatory. Amanda finally agreed, but again tried to back out when she was told that her mother would have to be present.

"Okay, I will take the physical and my mom can go, but don't tell her why," Amanda relented. Mrs. Stringer explained that her mother would have to be told everything and she had to be present during the examination.

"Okay, I have to leave now to make the arrangements for you to see a doctor today," Mrs. Stringer said. Amanda asked if Mona and Anne could stay with her for a while at the school until it was time for her to go home.

Mrs. Stringer then called Melissa at work and made arrangements to meet with her during her lunch break.

"Listen, Mrs. Jenkins, these are extremely serious allegations. I must have Amanda examined. I have made an appointment for her to see Dr. Snyder this afternoon."

"I tell you what, this is crazy and them allegations are plum ridiculous! She ain't seeing no damn doctor unless both me and my husband are there with her! I think I know where Tom is. I'm going right now to get him and I'll back here in a half hour," said Melissa defiantly.

After Melissa hung up, Mrs. Stringer called the Athens Police department to inquire about Tom's criminal history.

"Yes ma'am, he does have a history," the records clerk responded.

"He has a DUI, he's been arrested for fighting, and he has one child abuse arrest." Mrs. Stringer pressed her for more details

63

about the child abuse case. The clerk explained that a sixteen-year-old boy was playing basketball in the street and he ran into the Jenkins children who were playing close by. Tom was watching the children from his house. When he saw the teenager approach the kids, he ran outside and beat him up. The clerk said Tom was charged with child abuse but the charges were later dropped for some reason.

Mrs. Stringer called the school to speak with the principal Mr. Fletcher to make sure all was well at the school. Mr. Fletcher told her that Mrs. Jenkins had come to the school while he was at lunch and took Amanda out of the school.

"Strange thing is, she left Robert here," Mr. Fletcher said pensively.

Mrs. Stringer called the regional office for advice as to what she should do in this situation. Her supervisor advised her that in view of the abuse she had uncovered, she should file a petition with the judge to seize the child.

Mrs. Stringer had to wait almost an hour on Judge Vaughn. He was teaching a class at the community college. When she finally caught up with him, he immediately agreed to sign an emergency order to seize Amanda based on Mrs. Stringer's account of events.

Shortly after Mrs. Stringer had obtained Judge Vaughn's agreement to sign the order, Melissa Jenkins called and told her she had picked up Amanda from school and she and her husband had to deliver a load of wood, but they were all home now. Mrs. Stringer sent an associate to the Jenkins residence and found they were not there. Mrs. Stringer couldn't understand why they had lied about their location.

Mrs. Stringer called Dr. Snyder to confirm Amanda's appointment for later that day. While they were talking on the phone, Melissa called on another line to say they would not be taking Amanda to see Dr. Snyder. Mrs. Stringer put the doctor's office on hold.

"Mrs. Jenkins, you don't have a choice!" she yelled. "You need to take her there right now. I want to know why you picked her up from school."

"She is my child, and don't you think for a minute that you're going to dictate to me how to raise my kids!" Melissa exclaimed.

"Let me ...," Melissa hung up before Mrs. Stringer could respond. She slammed the phone on to the counter. "That bitch!" Yelled Mrs. Stringer in frustration.

She picked up the other line and the doctor's receptionist was waiting, "Listen, I'm sorry but I have to cancel that appointment. Tell Dr. Snyder I said thank you."

Melissa Jenkins called back and told Mrs. Stringer that she and her husband were taking Amanda to a doctor of their choice. Mrs. Stringer was furious and screamed over the phone telling Melissa that her actions were totally unacceptable. Mrs. Stringer thought for a second then asked, "All right, who is the doctor?"

"That ain't none of your business and I want you to know we just hired us an attorney." Melissa yelled. Mrs. Stringer could hear Tom Jenkins in the background saying things like, "Fuck her, it ain't none of her damn business! She needs to stop harassing us and our young'uns Melissa hung up.

Less than an hour passed and Melissa and Amanda entered the Human Services office. Mrs. Stringer greeted her in the lobby and Melissa handed her two statements from two different doctors. The first written by Dr. L.H. McMullen said, "I found no evidence of sexual intercourse." The second statement written by Dr. Ellen Wells read, "This certifies that I found no evidence of sexual intercourse."

Mrs. Stringer immediately called Dr. Wells who stated she had conducted a rectal exam but was unable to even insert her finger into Amanda's vagina. Therefore, she stopped the examination at that point, stating, "I knew at that point this child hasn't had any type of sexual activity."

"How the hell can you make a statement like that? How do you know there hasn't been some other type of contact?" Mrs. Stringer challenged her.

"Don't question my integrity, Mrs. Stringer. I have been a doctor for a long time and I know what I'm doing."

Amanda was sitting in the lobby chair, looking dejectedly at the floor. She slowly stood up, her hands and legs shaking, and said. "Mrs. Stringer, I lied about all that stuff. I just didn't want Anne to think I was a liar." Amanda never once raised her head as she made this statement. Then she turned and walked out.

Melissa turned to Mrs. Stringer, "You need to stop harassing my children at school!"

"Let me explain one thing to you, Mrs. Jenkins. I have all the authority in the world to talk to your children. All my actions have been supported by the District Attorney and the Juvenile Judge! Regardless of what your doctors reported, your children had severe and questionable bruises on them".

Melissa was completely silent for a few seconds before blurting out, "I'm so damn sick of this. These are my kids and me and their daddy will discipline them the way we see fit, and it ain't none of your business!"

Just as Melissa was about to walk out, Mrs. Stringer yelled in a loud authoritative tone, "Mrs. Jenkins!

Melissa stopped and looked back.

"How can you permit this man to beat and torture your children? He's not even their father!"

Melissa became extremely hostile at this outburst and began directing obscenities at Mrs. Stringer.

Melissa slammed the door and marched out. Then, as an afterthought, she re-opened it, stuck her head out and said, "For your information, Amanda has had sex before with boys her own age.

Mrs. Stringer was quite shocked and responded, "If Amanda has had sex with boys her own age, then why did that doctor say there was no sign of sexual contact?"

Mrs. Stringer stopped by Judge Vaughn's chambers and asked if he had signed the petition. The Judge paused for a minute and said, with some reluctance, "Mrs. Stringer, my attorney just talked to Dr. Wells and due to the contents of her report, I can no longer sign this petition."

"You can't cancel it now!" Mrs. Stringer exclaimed in despair.

"This is ridiculous, Judge Vaughn. You have got to let me remove that child until we can positively determine there has been no sexual abuse. Judge, there is more than one way to sexually abuse a child other than actual intercourse!"

"What the hell are you on here, Mrs. Stringer, a witch hunt?" the judge asked accusingly.

"Judge, I can't believe what I'm hearing here. What's going on?
Let's just take the kids while we investigate these allegations. This man could kill these children," Mrs. Stringer pleaded.

The judge told her he had heard enough. "There isn't enough evidence to support this petition, so I am canceling it. That's my final decision."

"What do you need? Two dead children?"

"I think you have said enough," the Judge said and turned his attention to a document on his desk.

"But Judge, what about the bruises and welts?" Mrs. Stringer continued. With that, the judge dismissed her from his office.

Mrs. Stringer immediately called her supervisor in Knoxville and explained what just happened. "There ain't no way that woman could have taken Amanda to those doctors," she complained.

67

"From the time we talked on the phone until she came in with those reports, only 45 minutes had lapsed. They're lying!" You want to know what I think? I think someone paid those doctors and that judge," Mrs. Stringer declared.

"You need to be very careful when making accusations like that," advised the Supervisor. Mrs. Stringer asked what she should do. Her supervisor referred her back to the multi-disciplinary team.

CHAPTER 23
Don't Tell

When Amanda and her mother arrived home, Tom and Robert were already there.

"You know he's going to kill me, mom!" Amanda yelled at her mother.

"Nah, he ain't going to kill ya. That man loves you and Robert."

As soon as they walked in the front door, they hear Tom's ear-splitting, belligerent voice booming out, "You think you are damn something, don't you? You damn little fucking bitch! You know I told you to keep your mother-fucking mouth shut. But you had to open your trap and embarrass me and your momma."

He looked over at Melissa and lowered his voice, suddenly sounding almost calm,. "Will you excuse us for a minute or two, Melissa? me and Amanda need to have a father and daughter discussion."

Amanda was sitting on the sofa and Tom moved in closer to her. His nose was touching Amanda's nose. He reached up and clutched her hair in his hand. He forced Amanda's head to turn upward so she was facing the ceiling.

"Now listen to me you fucking little whore, there ain't no social worker ever going to fuck me over. And you better learn one mother-fucking thing, young lady. Nobody will ever testify against me in this town, or any other town. You have seriously fucked up, Amanda Jenkins. You have really fucked up!" Tom's face was now beet-red and he was screaming so hard, Amanda couldn't understand the words.

He took the back side of his hand and struck Amanda on the head above the hair line. He continued holding on to her hair. He adjusted his grip, grabbing the hair on the back of her head above her neck. The pain he was inflicting on Amanda was excruciating. Amanda was trying not to cry out loud, but tears were streaming down her face. He slapped her again on the top of her head. He grabbed Amanda between her legs and squeezed his hand together almost inserting his fingers into her vagina through her pants. He was continuing to pull on her hair. He forced her to bend way backwards and then released her, causing her to drop to the floor.

"I just don't fucking understand you. I love you and I take care of you, but I told you I would kill you and your little brother if you ever said anything."

He called out to Robert, "Robert, get in here." As Robert entered the living room, Tom stood up and kneed him in the groin. Robert bent over and started crying. Poor Robert had no idea why he was just kneed. Robert fell onto the floor and Tom bellowed, "You know what I think? I think I'm going to have to kill you. And it's your sister's fault, son."

"You are making me kill my son! You bitch!" he screeched at Amanda.

"It's not my fault!" Amanda sobbed.

Tom opened a drawer and removed a 38-caliber revolver. He turned away from Amanda and Robert and removed the bullets. "Now we are going to play a little game." He pretended he just put a bullet into the gun and spun the cylinder with the palm of his hand.

"Okay, who's first?" Tom glared first at Amanda, then Robert.

Amanda shrieked, "NO, NO, NO." Tom grabbed Robert by his hair and pulled close to him.

"Watch this, Amanda. Watch close. Maybe you will get to see your brother's brains splatter all over the wall." Robert pulled away hysterically trying to break free. Tom pointed the revolver at Robert's head and counted, "One, two ...," Amanda interrupted and shrieked, louder this time, "NO! NO! Do me. Do me!" Tom began counting again, "one, two, three." he pulled the trigger. The gun snapped and the hammer fell forward. Robert jerked as the hammer fell. Amanda let out a blood curdling scream.

"Okay you lucked out that time, Robert. It's your turn now, Amanda," Tom whispered threateningly. Amanda tried to stand up and run but Tom tackled her. He held her down on her back and straddled her chest.

"Okay, here goes. Will you be as lucky as your little brother? Robert turned away crying but Tom grabbed his head and forced him to watch. Tom put the barrel of the gun in Amanda's mouth and said,

"One, two …," he pulled the hammer back and then said, "Three! The hammer slammed forward. Amanda jerked and blinked her eyes.

Tom stood up and put Robert next to Amanda. "Now you listen to me! I'm not going to kill you. hell, I love you two very much, but other people won't understand our situation!

If anyone ever comes again and tells me we got problems in our family, I won't be so nice next time. You both know now that there ain't nothing going to happen when you talk to those people. Do you believe that now?"

Tom glared into their eyes with a cruel, terrifying gaze. "Do you believe I am more powerful than those people?" Both Robert and Amanda meekly muttered, "Yes." Tom quickly came back with "Yes, Sir!"

Amanda and Robert repeated in tandem, "Yes, Sir!"

Tom sent them to their room. Robert and Amanda were both gasping for air the way one does after a hard cry. Robert's nose was running.

Robert said, "Amanda, Con…!"

"Shh …" Amanda said, cutting him off. "Just calm down" as she attempted to comfort her little brother.

"Amanda, I don't want to live no more. I don't want to. I just want to die."

"Robert, it won't be forever, I promise. We are going to grow up and it will all be over then"

Robert looked up sadly at Amanda, "what if we don't grow up? What if he doesn't let us? I am afraid. I am real scared"

They both lay in the room crying until they fell asleep.

Mrs. Stringer wrote up her report and submitted it to the multi-disciplinary team, a group of Human Services professionals that reviewed these types of cases and made recommendations for further action to the State.

The team recommended that the parents (Tom and Melissa) be told what actions had been taken to this point by the department, with a full explanation why these procedures must be followed. Additionally, the team recommended that Amanda be provided professional help.

"When a child makes up these kinds of stories, it indicates there is a serious problem," the team stated in its report. "I think it's necessary to have the parents take courses focused on effective discipline and understanding of juvenile problems," one team member suggested.

A new investigator Mrs. Croft was assigned to the case. Mrs. Croft called the Jenkins' residence and spoke with Melissa. She heard Tom cursing in the background. Suddenly, Tom grabbed the phone and screamed, "you know you have a lot of fucking nerve calling this house again!" Mrs. Croft explained that this was just a follow-up visit and she would not take too much of their time. Tom reluctantly agreed to an appointment and she set a date and time to visit their home.

"Mr. and Mrs. Jenkins, I think you should consider some counseling for Amanda," Mrs. Croft gently advised them during her visit.

"Mrs. Croft," Melissa said, "both my husband and I have spoken to Amanda about this whole mess. She told us she was just upset because she was not allowed to spend the night at Anne's house. "

"Well, if you don't think she would benefit from counseling, I will let the team know you're not interested."

"Good," Tom responded. "Then we can all rest easier

CHAPTER 24

Starting a Logging Business

It was the fall of 1979 and the mountains were once again ablaze with yellow, orange and gold. Tom and Gene Cawthorn were chatting at work.

"I am so sick and tired of working in this wood yard," Tom complained. Both were working for a wood mill in Southern Tennessee.

"I work my ass off for nothing," Tom said.

"I second that," agreed Gene

"Why don't we start our own damn outfit?" Tom suggested

"Cost too much Tom. Hell, it would run perty near $20,000 to get started, and we ain't got nothing."

"Well, let's go to the bank and borrow the money. That's what we will do. Let's form a partnership and haul our own damn logs."

"Yes, sir. we've both been in the business for more than 10 years. We know the business backwards and forwards," Gene boasted to the loan officer.

"Well, I can't give you an answer right now, boys. I have to take it to the board of directors for their decision. You know, it might take until the end of the week. I'll call ya when they've made a decision."

"Damn, I want that loan," Tom said. "Shit, we got it." Gene said, his confidence growing.

"I think we've got it, too. Let's go celebrate," Tom said jubilantly.

"Bring us a beer, Millie." Tom yelled down to the end of the bar. The barmaid Millie looked up and saw it was Tom Jenkins making this order.

"Shit," she muttered to herself, every time this guy comes in we have trouble."

"Tom, you're going to behave in here tonight, ain't ya?" she demanded.

"Of course I am Millie. I always behave," he assured her.

"Rack 'em," Tom said to Gene. "You know I'm going to kick your ass in a game of eight ball."

Tom and Gene were playing their eighth game and Tom was on his tenth beer.

"Hey buddy, how about you two give it up for some other people to play?" asked a bar patron.

"Go to hell, asshole, I'll give it up when we're damn fucking ready," Tom bellowed.

"Kiss my ass man," replied the patron.

"Fuck you!" Tom said as he pushed the patron back at his chest. The bar patron bounced up and swung his right hand striking Tom in the jaw. Tom fell backwards on to the pool table and stood back up. His opponent picked up a pool stick and broke it in half. Tom put his right hand in his pocket and drew out a Barlow pocket knife. He opened the knife with a flick of his wrist. He had just recently sharpened the blade with an oiled-down Whetstone. It was razor sharp. The man put down the pool stick and said, "hey, I don't want no fucking trouble, man." He put his hands up and walked away.

"All right then!" Tom said as he placed the opened knife back into his pants pocket. The patron stuck out his right hand to shake hands with Tom.

"My name is Gordon." Tom grabbed his hand and pulled Gordon in a violent tug right up close to Tom's chest as Tom withdrew the knife from his pocket. Tom placed the blade of the knife against Gordon's neck.

"Hey man, don't do it, man, please man. I'm sorry, man, please, please!" he begged. Tom ran the blade down Gordon's throat as blood began to trickle from his neck.

"You ever fucking hit me again partner and I'll cut your fucking throat, you got that?"

"Yeah, buddy, I got that," Gordon replied.

"Now get the fuck out of my bar," Tom said. Gordon walked directly out of the bar.

"That bastard. I ain't finished with him. No sir, payback is hell," Gordon vowed to a friend.

Tom and Gene finished their last game and ordered one more beer for the road.

CHAPTER 25

No One is Home; Tom throws a fit

"Honey, I am home," called Tom, as he entered the trailer at 3:00 a.m.

No response.

"Where the fuck are you?" Tom checked the bedrooms but no one was around.

"Where are you?" he screamed again. "Damn it." Tom picked up the phone and called Melissa's mother, Ruth.

"Hello", came the sleepy voice at the other end of the phone. It was Ted, Melissa's younger brother. "Missy over there?" Tom asked.

"Tom, they're all sleeping." Ted hung up and Tom simply exploded. He ripped the phone out of the wall and ran out the door slamming it behind him.

He drove up to Ruth's house and honked the car horn. It was 4:00 a.m. Tom got out of the car, slamming the door shut, and took a baseball bat from the trunk of his car.

"Ted fucking Roberts, how dare you hang up on me? You stupid little bastard." By now the entire neighborhood was awake.

Ted's new Pontiac Grand Prix was parked in Ruth's driveway. "This is a mighty nice car you got here, Ted!" yelled Tom. He raised the bat high into the air and swung it right into the center of Ted's windshield.

"Now, what? Wanna hang up on me again, motherfucker?" He swung the bat again, this time at the driver's window, shattering the glass into the car.

"Melissa! Melissa! MELISSA!" His voice got louder each time he repeated her name, until he finally received a response.

"What, honey?" Melissa swung open the front door with both kids in her arms. "I am coming, baby. I was just visiting

Mamma and all of us fell asleep." Her voice was quivering with fear.

It was a quiet trip home. No one said a word. Robert and Amanda fell asleep in the back seat and Tom left them there when they got home.

Melissa was scared to death of Tom after he had been drinking, but in some twisted way, she enjoyed the violent sex with him. She enjoyed being dominated and ordered what to do, even if what she was doing was wrong and she knew it was taboo.

That night, Tom woke up in the middle of the night. He was sexually aroused, perhaps from a dream. He quietly slipped out of bed and walked into the living room. He was planning to watch a pornographic movie and masturbate. However, when he got into the living room, Robert was sitting on the sofa watching an "I Love Lucy" re-run.

"What are you doing up this late?"

Robert was startled and looked wide-eyed at Tom standing boldly in the living room with no clothes on. Tom did not attempt to hide his erection.

"Nothing, I couldn't sleep," Robert replied. Tom walked over to his video storage box and removed an X-rated movie. Robert sat there in his pajamas watching "I Love Lucy" trying to ignore Tom. Tom bent down in front of the television and inserted the videotape into a VCR.

"Robert, put it on channel 3."

"Yes, sir."

The TV screen switched to a man and woman noisily enjoying oral sex.

"Oh boy!" said Tom. He sat on the sofa next to Robert and started masturbating. "Here, Robert, you do it for me."

Tom grabbed Robert's hand and directed it to his penis. Robert did what he was told. Robert was also getting aroused watching the video. Tom noticed Robert's erection and told him to remove his pants. The next hour went on forever, with Tom giving oral sex to Robert and Robert having to provide the same for Tom. Tom sodomized Robert that evening and forced Robert to do the same on him.

CHAPTER 26

The Night of the Fish Fry

"Come on over, Amanda," Anne said. "Let's do something fun." Anne and Amanda were best friends. They both lived in the same trailer park. Anne and her mother lived in a trailer across the street and down to the right from Amanda's trailer. They were like sisters and were always together. If they weren't in Amanda's house, they were in Anne's house.

"You know, your mom and dad are like my second parents," Anne said to Amanda.

"You're my best friend, Anne,"

"We are best friends and we will always be together," Anne vowed.

"Did I tell you what mom got me yesterday?" She bought me an Easy Bake oven, but the light bulb that cooks the cake is blown out."

"As soon as we get another bulb, you and me can cook ourselves a cake," Anne said excitedly.

"Amanda, come on home!" Melissa called from the front door of their trailer. "Tom and me are going to a fish fry tonight and we're taking Anne's Momma with us. So Anne is going to stay here with you and Robert tonight. You bess behave now, you hear me?"

"We will, Mom. Don't worry," Amanda said.

The fish fry ended around 11:30 p.m. Tom and Melissa drove home with Anne's Mom in the back seat. Both Melissa and Tom were pretty intoxicated.

"Why don't you let Anne spend the night, Mona?" They're probably asleep already, don't you think?" said Melissa. They all agreed it would be best not to disturb them. So Tom and Melissa dropped Mona off at her trailer and parked next to their own.

Amanda, Robert and Anne were fast asleep in Amanda and Robert's bedroom. Tom and Melissa's loud conversation in the other bedroom awakened them.

Melissa came to their room. "We brought home some fried catfish." Melissa said. "Y'all get up and eat some."

Amanda, Robert and Anne all got up and sat down in front of the television watching a western movie, contentedly eating catfish and hush puppies and sipping on ice tea.

Tom and Melissa excused themselves from the living room and went back into their bedroom.

Amanda and Robert walked to Tom and Melissa's bedroom. Anne stood up and followed them in there. When she opened the door, she saw Tom lying on his back on the bed with his feet on the floor and Melissa performing oral sex on him. Anne went white and felt weak with shock. Amanda and Robert were acting as if nothing was happening. Anne shrieked, and ran back into Amanda's room.

Anne lay motionless on Amanda's bed, unsure what to make of what she had just seen. Then, the door opened and Melissa, in her nightgown, stood in the doorway.

"What are you doing?" Anne asked.

"Nothing, honey", Melissa whispered. Moments later Tom entered the room, wearing only his underwear. Anne sat up in bed and made an attempt to leave, but Melissa wouldn't let her out of the door.

"Go lay back down, honey," Melissa said, as she pushed Anne back on to the bed. Melissa put her weight on Anne and held her down while Tom pulled up her nightgown and removed her panties.

"Stop it!" Anne screamed. .

She was just too tiny and vulnerable and he was big and strong. Tom slipped into the twin bed and manipulated his way inside of her. Anne did not even let loose a whimper. Tom had his way with her. Melissa released her as soon as Tom was finished.

"If you say a word about this to anyone, young lady, I will kill you, do you understand me?" Tom whispered menacingly.

"Yes sir!" Anne could barely speak – she was in shock and emotionally drained.

Anne jumped up from the bed and ran into the bathroom. She was hurting mentally and physically, and so embarrassed. She was just 12 years old. Tom followed her into the bathroom.

"It wasn't so bad, was it, honey?"

"I have to go home, Mr. Jenkins!" Anne could barely speak through the tears just flowing – she was confused and scared.

"Nope, I think you better hang around for a while. Your mom won't understand you coming home in the middle of the night," said Tom. "Come on with me." He grabbed her hand and led her into his and Melissa's bedroom. Anne was totally mortified as she looked in. Melissa was having oral sex with Robert. "He is only 8 or 9 years old", she thought.

Tom made her stand up against the wall and watch. She watched in horror as Tom had sex with Amanda and Melissa performed oral sex, first on Robert, and then Amanda.

"My God!" She thought. "What is happening here? Why are they doing that?" Anne slid down the wall and sat on the floor in the corner of the room, turning her head away to hide the shame. But she wasn't able to block out the noise of the incestuous orgy. Anne left the house at 6:00 a.m., explaining to their mother that she had had a bad dream and wanted to come home early.

In the weeks to follow, Anne asked Amanda why this had happened. Amanda replied that it happens all the time,

"But you can't tell anyone about it, you can't tell anyone ever, please. It's our secret, okay? He would kill me and Robert if I ever said anything to anybody.

Promise me you won't say anything."

"I have to tell someone, I just have to, Amanda," Anne was in anguish.

81

One afternoon several weeks later, Anne heard someone calling her from outside.

"Get out here, Anne! Get out here right now!" It was Elizabeth Roberts, Melissa's little sister. "I'm going to kick your ass all over this yard. You have a big mouth bitch and I am going to shut it for you." Anne walked outside. "What are you talking about?" she said.

Elizabeth jumped on her and started swinging her fist, striking Anne on her chest, her back and in the face. Anne grabbed at Elizabeth's hair and pulled as hard as she could.

"You better keep your fucking mouth shut, bitch!" Elizabeth screamed. "You were told not to tell anyone!"

"Tell what?" Anne asked desperately as Elizabeth straddled her, holding down her shoulders and arms.

"Amanda told you not to tell anyone. So you better not, do you understand?"

As she struck Anne in the face with a closed fist, Anne's mother ran outside and broke up the fight.

"Get off her, you filthy pig," Anne's mother screeched.

CHAPTER 27

Starting a Logging Business

Later the next morning, the phone in Tom's trailer rang.

"Hello," said Tom as he picked up the phone. "That's great Mr. Klein. You just made my day!" Tom cried jubilantly. "$20,000 will get us a used truck, some new chain saws, and a wrench," Tom thought.

"Yes sir, sure we can, we'll both be down there in thirty minutes." Tom exclaimed, acting like an excited schoolboy.

"We got it, damn it! We got it, Gene," Tom said over the phone.

"Meet me at the bank in 30 minutes, partner," Tom said.

"I'm on the way," Gene cheerfully replied.

"Sign here, here and here," the loan officer said as he pointed to the X's marked on the loan agreement. Both Tom and Gene signed and the loan officer extended his hand.

"Congratulations gentlemen and good luck," he said as he shook both their hands and handed Tom a check for $20,000.

"Okay, so we agree that Melissa will be our bookkeeper, right?" Tom said eagerly to Gene as they left the bank.

"Well, okay," Gene responded with some hesitation, "but let's first agree on our salaries and how we split the income."

"$300 each per week, the rest goes into the bank and pays the loan, how's that?" Tom replied.

"Sounds fair to me," Gene said.

"Yes, sir! I think this truck will do just fine," Tom said as he slammed the door on a 1963 Mac tractor. We need a log trailer though, and a winch."

It was almost noon on a mid-summer's day, and both Tom and Gene were deep in the woods cutting timber. The sun was beating down on them.

"Watch out for copperheads," Gene warned as he pulled some brush away from a pine tree trunk.

"Shit!" Tom screamed, as a copperhead launched a lightning fast strike at his work boots. He swung at the snake with the bow of his chain saw and flipped the snake up into the air.

"Damn it, Tom, you trying to kill me?" Gene yelled. The snake slithered off silently under a pile of tree branches.

"I think this tree is too big, Tom," Gene said as they surveyed a huge natural pine. It must have been three and half feet in diameter and sitting right on the edge of a 30 or 40 foot drop off.

"I want this tree," Tom replied determinedly. "That's big money. Go get the truck and let's tie a cable around it right here," he said, pointing to a spot on the tree about eight feet over his head.

"Maybe we can keep it from going over that cliff," Tom said. Gene backed the truck up and began releasing cable from the winch. "How's that?" Gene yelled. "That enough?"

"Just a little more cable," Tom replied. Sweat was rolling off his forehead.

"Okay, draw up some tension," Tom yelled, as he started up his chain saw. "All right, get ready," his voice rising in volume as his tension rose.

He pressed the twirling chain against the base of the tree. It was tearing out pieces of pine, spitting it out in all directions. The sawdust covered Tom's head and blanketed his shirt. The sound of the saw was deafening. Tom had to switch to the other side of the tree.

"Tom! Don't get between the truck and tree," Gene yelled. But it was too late. At that moment the trunk and tree separated with a thunderous crack. The cable snapped and almost slid off at the base of the tree, jerking it towards the truck. Tom was pinned between the rear wheels and the jagged cut. The chain saw fell to the ground running at top speed. It continued to dance and bounce on the ground and it was only inches from Tom's right side, kicking up dirt and rocks all over his back. Gene jumped down from the truck and reached for the handle of the saw. It kicked back as it the chain dug into the ground. Gene fell backwards and the chain saw dropped over the cliff, stopping only upon impact.

"You okay Tom? Tom you okay? answer me!" Gene thought the worst. Tom was pinned tight against the wheel. A knot on the tree was pushing against his chest.

"I can't breathe," Tom mumbled. The top of the tree was hanging over the cliff with the base pinned underneath the back-end of the truck. There was so much weight on the truck that the back tires were suspended in the air and not touching the ground.

"I don't know what to do Tom," Gene cried out in despair.

I can't move the truck. The wheels ain't touching the fucking ground, Tom."

Gene surveyed the scene and quickly summed up the situation. "If I release the cable, that tree is going to crush you to death."

At that moment, a breeze kicked up and the tree began to sway in the wind. Tom was in intense pain. The tree knot had ruptured his chest. It looked like a rib was being pushed into his heart.

"I'm dying," Tom said in a weak, hoarse voice. He lost consciousness and his head fell toward the ground.

"Oh shit", Gene screamed, "Help, Help!" His screams were drowned by the noise of the wind blowing through the trees.

Gene ran to his pickup truck. His lights were on.

"Oh no" he thought to himself. "The battery is going to be dead."

Holding his breath and saying a silent prayer, he inserted the key and turned it. To his huge relief, the engine turned over and cranked.

"Thank you God," he prayed out loud.

Gene pulled up to the gas station. His truck was overheating and the brakes were smoking. He ran inside, breathing hard and gasping for air.

"Call the Sheriff," he said, "Its Tom, he's pinned under the truck.

He needs help FAST." Gene struggled to get the words out in between his gasps for air.

"Where?" Paul asked.

"Go to the power line and make a right. We're about three miles down at the cliff," he screamed.

"I got to go back. I think we need some trucks with winches," he ordered as he slammed the door shut on his pickup truck. His tires squealed and white smoke bellowed from underneath them, as he sped off.

"His blood pressure is normal and his pulse is 84," a paramedic reported.

"Okay, you're going to have to pull the base of the log out towards the right. Okay slow," Gene screamed.

"Oohhh," Tom moaned as the weight gradually was lifted from his chest.

"He's got a sucking chest wound. Get me some plastic and a wrap. Hurry!" the paramedic yelled,

Tom was loaded into the ambulance. Gene rode with him in the back.

"His prognosis is very good," the doctor in the emergency room told Melissa. He has a cracked rib, but that's about the extent of it. We'll keep him overnight and he can go home tomorrow",

"Thank God," she said. "I was so worried."

Eight months after the accident, Tom was back to normal and Tom and Gene were in the woods again. They were still using the old fashioned winch on the truck to pull the logs onto the trailer.

"This is bullshit," Tom said. "We need a front-end loader." The next morning, they both headed back to the bank to apply for another loan for a front-end loader. The bank loan officer explained their credit was not good enough.

"Your company has been late on almost every payment since you went into business. We just can't do it this time. Only way you boys could get more money would be if you had a co-signer."

As Gene and Tom walked dejectedly out of the bank, Gene asked, "What does he mean we have been late on all our payments?"

"Hell, it hasn't been easy!" Tom yelled. They sat down in the truck and Gene pressed Tom again for an explanation as to why the company had been late making payments.

"I agreed to let you and Melissa keep the books and make the payments, but if you ain't doing it, I need to take over," Gene exclaimed.

"Fuck you, Gene Cawthorn. There ain't nothing wrong with our finances," Tom said.

"I hold on to our money until the last minute so we can make money off the interest," Tom explained.

They sat in the truck for a while, both men deep in thought.

"What about your daddy-in-law? Do you think he would co-sign for us to buy the loader?" asked Tom

Gene shook his head and said he wouldn't even think of asking.

"Well, damn it, Gene. What do you want? You want us to go out of fucking business? That's what's going to happen if we don't get a loader," Tom screamed. "Now, are you going to talk to him? Or do I need to call the man?"

Gene agreed to call, but made it clear to Tom how things would be if his father-in-law co-signed, "If you have to be late on any payment, don't be late on the one with my daddy-in-law's name on it. He's getting old and can't afford to have his credit ruined, is that clear?" said Gene defiantly.

CHAPTER 28

The Business Needs More Money

Gene put the call into his dad-in-law, "Listen Dad, our business is going real good and all that, but we need a loader."

Gene's dad-in-law had always had a soft spot for his favorite son-in-law. "All right, I'll help you boys out."

The next morning, Gene's father-in-law accompanied the two of them to the bank. He co-signed the loan to borrow money and tom purchase a front-end loader. As they were leaving the bank he said,

"Boys I got faith in you now, don't let me down, 'cause I ain't got the money to pay back this loan."

Some time passed and Jenkins & Cawthorn Logging had acquired more equipment. Gene and his wife applied for a loan using their home as collateral.

"Tom we've been doing damn well lately. I think we both deserve a raise. What we're getting right now just ain't doing it," Gene said, speaking with both Tom and Melissa.

"Not yet," Tom said. "This way we are paying more towards the loan. Soon we will be making big bucks."

"Tom, I can't wait. I have loans with my bank and I've got bills to pay. I'll tell you what. There's a construction company here in Athens and I can make more just working for them," Gene said.

"Okay, Go! Get the fuck out! You do what you got to do, Gene." Tom said.

"Damn, we're bringing in upward of $3,000.00 a week, Tom. I just want my share, shit!" Gene reasoned. "You want this damn company? I'll just sign it over to you, lock stock and barrel."

"That's fine with me. You make the arrangements and I will sign the papers." Tom replied.

"Just remember one fucking thing, it's all mine. You get nothing for backing out on me."

"You know you got to make it good Tom. Margaret's father is up to his ears in debt financing our equipment and I got a personal loan," Gene said. Margaret was Gene's wife and her father had helped the two of them purchase more equipment since their first loan.

Two months later, Gene made a phone call to Tom.

"Tom, listen to me, man, I got the papers. You need to meet with me so we can sign" Gene said.

"Okay, Gene I'll meet you after work at the club," Tom said.

"What time?" Gene asked. "Make it 7:00 p.m.," Tom replied.

"Honey, I got Tom to agree to meet me. He is going to sign the papers this afternoon," Gene told his wife over the phone.

"Thank God, Gene, because he ain't making no payments on nothing.

You know that Melissa Jenkins used one of the company checks at the grocery store," Margaret said. "The banks are going to come after us if you don't get them papers signed."

"What time is it, Millie?" Gene asked the bartender.

"It's 8:45, Gene, why?" asked Millie.

"Oh nothing," Gene replied. Gene waited for two hours and finally left the bar.

"Honey, I waited until 9:00 p.m. and he didn't show up," Gene told his wife.

"You're a fucking pussy, Gene!" She yelled.

"You're fucking afraid to stand up to that bastard, why?" she yelled again.

"I guess I am, honey, I have never told you this but, more than once he has gotten mad at me in the woods and beat the hell out of me"

"He what? When? Why haven't you ever told me this before, Gene?" Margret asked.

"Remember that night I came home with a bruise on my face, I told you a log broke loose for the cable and hit me?" Gene asked.

"Yes, I remember," replied Margaret,

"It was Tom he got mad at me 'cause I was too slow backing up the front-end loader. He yelled at me, called me a piece of shit and dragged me out the truck. Then he hauled off and hit me with a tree limb," Gene explained. "Shit, not long after his accident we got into a fight in woods. Son of bitch left me out there with no ride. I had to walk six miles out the highway and hitch a ride into town."

"He is one sorry bastard," Margaret said,

"Just get him to sign the papers so we ain't responsible no more," Margaret said, as she closed the bedroom door behind her.

CHAPTER 29
Tom Gets Shot (1979)

"None of the damn tires on that truck are worth a shit," Tom grumbled while he was changing a rear truck tire. "This stupid thing split while the truck was in woods."

"You wouldn't think your own old man would rip you off," he said as he spoke with Paul at the gas station.

"Put this wheel in there," Tom said, pointing to a device Paul had built to make changing the big truck tires a little safer.

"That motherfucker ripped me off!" Tom yelled out loud. I'm going to get my money back, that's for damn sure."

He left the gas station with a six pack of beer on his front seat. He drove the truck back to the wood yard and sat there until he finished all six beers. The longer he sat there thinking about the tires, the more furious he became with his father.

"Open the damn door Tim," Tom yelled, as he banged on his father's front door. "Open the fucking door!"

"What the fuck do you want Tom Jenkins? It's fucking 2:30 in the damn morning," his father called down.

"I want my money for those crappy-ass tires you sold me," Tom screamed out.

"I ought to kick your ass, for waking me up for that," Tim replied. Tom was known around town for being a mean son-of-a-bitch, but to be as mean as his father you have to multiply Tom by ten. Tim was ruthless, and infamous for pulling a knife on anyone who stood his or her ground with him.

"You just bess make it right with me, right fucking now, Dad, or I'm going to have to kick your fucking ass, old man!" Tom screamed. While Tom was talking, he pulled open the squeaky screen door. Tim was standing not more than two or three feet from him as Tom was talking, and he balled up his fist and threw a demoralizing blow to Tom's head. Tom fell back and tripped over an ottoman falling onto the floor.

"You bastard, I'll kill you old man!" Tom threatened. He stood up, shook it off, and grabbed a rusty old rod iron fire poker that was leaning up against the wood stove. He swung that poker with everything he had. Tim ducked but the poker made contact skimming the top of head. Tim didn't say a word. He lunged at Tom and head-butted him in the forehead. Tom fell through the screen door, out onto the wooden porch

"You stay the fuck out of my house, you worthless piece of dog shit," Tim screamed out as he slammed the door. Tim was into his kitchen when Tom burst back through the door, but this time he had a gun in his hand, it was 25-caliber chrome-plated automatic.

"What you going to do with that?" Tim yelled out.

"You going to kill your ole man?" Tim yelled. Tom raised the gun, pointing it at his father's chest. Tim swung his fist at Tom's hand and knocked the gun free. Both Tom and Tim scrambled to gain procession of the gun. They fell onto the wood stove, knocking it over. Ashes and a cloud of black soot filled the room. Tim got his hands on the gun first. Tom jumped onto his back and tried to grab his hand. Tim tucked his hand underneath his own body and then Tom picked up a section of stovepipe and struck Tim in the head. The pipe was thin and not very heavy. Tim turned around and had the gun in his right hand pointing it at Tom.

"Now get on your damn feet," Tim yelled, with some difficulty since he was out of breath and covered in soot. Tom stood there panting and breathing hard, as well.

"You know what you need, you worthless piece of dog shit?" Tim asked. He pointed the gun at Tom's right leg.

"What the hell are you doing?" Tom screamed. Tim pulled the trigger discharging the weapon, shooting Tom in the leg.

"You shot me, are you fucking crazy?" Tom yelled out.

"That's right, now get out of my house and don't you ever come back this way, you hear me?" Tim yelled. Tom limped out defeated and bleeding.

"You remember one thing boy, I shot you in the leg. I could have killed you or shot you in a bone, but I didn't," Tim said.

When Tom walked in the door of his home he looked like a coal miner. His clothes, face, arms and hands were black from the wood stove ashes and soot. "If he wasn't my ole man I would have killed the bastard," Tom told Melissa, as she cleaned his wounds.

"You bess go down to the emergency room and have 'em look at this gunshot wound." Melissa said.

"Naw, I'll be all right. The bullet went clean through. Just put some iodine on it with this here," he said bravely as he handed Melissa a cotton swab.

CHAPTER 30

Don't Hide the Hair Brush

Months passed and Tom's wounds had healed. Melissa was cleaning the trailer with the assistance of both Robert and Amanda.

"Where's my hairbrush?" Tom asked in an irritated tone

"I don't know where it is," Melissa answered.

"Do you know Amanda?" Tom asked.

"Nope," Amanda responded.

Tom began looking throughout the trailer turning over couch pillows and at one point kneeling to look under the sofa.

"I wish people would leave my shit alone," Tom yelled out in anger.

"Okay everybody stop what you're doing and find my fucking brush," he yelled.

Amanda started looking in kitchen drawers and Melissa went back to search the bedroom. Robert didn't move. He just sat on the ottoman watching television.

Tom was getting extremely angry and started throwing things around the house.

Robert reached under the ottoman and to his surprise, he found the hairbrush. Amanda walked over to Robert and he handed her the brush.

"Here it is Tom," Amanda said.

"Was you holding on to that brush all this time?" Tom screamed. I been looking all over this damn house and you knew all along where it was?"

"No sir, I didn't know where it was" Amanda responded.

"Damn it. Yes, you did," Tom yelled violently as he lifted his hand over his head with the brush in it. He swung and struck

Robert on top of his head making the brush break in half. Robert dropped to the floor and started crying. Tom took the broken end of the brush and hit Amanda on the top of her head. He hit her so hard that a knot popped up on her head immediately after he hit her.

"Now look what you made me do," he yelled. "Now I done broke my fucking brush,"

"Melissa, your kids are a pain in my ass," Tom yelled.

CHAPTER 31

A Florida Vacation

"You think we should make a reservation before we take off to Daytona?" Melissa asked Tom.

"Hell, no. We can find something when we get there," Tom said.

"We're going to let Elizabeth come with us, right?" Melissa asked.

"I reckon," Tom replied.

"All right, did we get everything? Make sure," Melissa cautioned.

"Robert, you got to go pee go now, you too, Amanda. I ain't stopping until we get to Florida," Tom barked.

Tom pulled the car up to Ruth's house and honked the horn. Elizabeth ran out with her suitcase. Tom got out of the car and opened the trunk.

"Put it here," he said. Minutes later they were on their way to Daytona Beach, Florida. They stopped at a Holiday Inn just down form the boardwalk and rented a room.

Tom was lying on the bed and yelled, "Damn it! Can you shut up? I am trying to relax." All the kids were begging to go swimming at the beach. Tom told them that after driving so long he needed to rest a little while.

"Come on, let's go!" cried Robert. Everyone was crowded into the small motel room.

"This room ain't big enough," Tom said.

"It's okay with me," said Melissa.

Tom told Melissa to take the kids to the beach so he could rest for a little while. So Melissa and the kids left and Tom fell fast asleep. Nearly three hours passed and Tom woke up in the room all alone. He stood up thinking how nice it was to enjoy some peace and tranquility.

"I need a drink," he thought. He left the motel room and walked to an ABC liquor store located in a small strip center just down the street from the Holiday Inn. He placed a bottle of rum and a two-liter bottle of coke on to the counter.

"You need any ice, sir?" The clerk asked.

"No, just this," Tom replied.

Tom returned to the motel room and mixed himself a drink. He turned the thermostat down on the air conditioner and the air conditioning unit kicked on.

Minutes later, his silence is broken. "We're back," Melissa said cheerfully as she opened the motel room door.

Elizabeth yelled out that she wanted to go skating.

"There is a roller rink down the street."

"Can we go skating?" asked Amanda.

"Yeah, I reckon," Tom replied.

"Let's drop them off at the roller rink, and we can go to the dog track," Tom suggested.

"What time is the last session?" Tom asked the roller rink attendant. He told the kids that he and Melissa would return at 10:00 p.m. to pick them up.

Tom and Melissa went to the dog track but had terrible luck betting on the greyhounds.

"Hell, let's go before we lose any more money," Tom said. They left the dog track and stopped by the liquor store to buy daiquiri mix and a bag of ice.

"Let's go get the kids and then we can relax with some ice-cold drinks" Tom told Melissa.

It was 11:00 p.m. and everyone was packed into the motel room. Tom and Melissa were drinking ice cold daiquiris and watching TV. Elizabeth got up from the bed and walked into the bathroom. Amanda followed her in there. They had had a good time at the rink and she wanted to discuss the details of their evening.

"Did you see that boy in the red shirt?" Elizabeth asked.

"Yes I did," Amanda giggled.

"What the hell you two doing in there?" Tom yelled out.

"Nutt'n, Dad" we're just talking." Amanda said grinning to Elizabeth. Tom opened the bathroom door and slammed it against the bathtub.

"What the hell are you talking about in here?" He drunkenly mumbled.

"What kind of shit are you telling Amanda?" Tom asked. Elizabeth said they were just talking about a boy they saw at the roller rink.

"You liar," Tom said. He threw his half-full glass of daiquiri at Elizabeth, hitting her just above her right eye.

"I am so tired of you fucking kids always lying," Tom yelled. He drew back his hand and slapped Elizabeth in the face with his open hand. Elizabeth started crying hysterically and Tom struck her again. Blood was running down the side of her head. Amanda moved out the way, went back to the double bed, and laid down burying herself under the bedspread and blanket.

"Why don't you act like you're 12 years old, instead of acting like you're fucking five?" Tom yelled. "I can't have a decent vacation with you kids around!"

"Melissa, call the Greyhound station and see what it would cost to send the three of 'em back home," Tom exclaimed.

"Tom I ain't going to do that."

"You ain't going to what?" he snapped back. "I told you to call the fucking bus station."

Melissa called information and obtained the number.

99

"Yes, ma'am. I want to know what it would cost to send three kids to Tennessee from here," she asked. All the kids were horrified at the thought that Tom was going to send them home on a bus.

Melissa packed Amanda's; Elizabeth's and Robert's clothes and told Amanda to take the bags to the car. The children were crying and begging to be allowed to stay. Tom and Melissa loaded the kids into the car and drove them to the Greyhound station.

"We don't want to go home!" Amanda told Tom. Tom got out of the car and walked purposefully into the Greyhound station. The kids were crying and pleading with him as he walked away.

No more than five minutes passed and Tom returned to the car.

"You know what I am going to do with you three?" Tom asked.

"No, what?" Amanda asked anxiously.

He sat down behind the wheel and drove back to the motel room.

"Everybody, bring your bags back in. I'm going to let you stay." Tom told the kids. All three were delighted. When they were all back in the room, Tom made an announcement.

"I am going to make you drink the rest of this rum." Melissa told him not to do that, but he had already made up his mind.

He made each of them sit down at the foot of the bed. Elizabeth said she was not going to do it and Tom yelled at her.

"Shut the fuck up, Elizabeth!" He began pouring rum into three plastic cups.

"Here," he said as he handed each kid a full glass of rum. "Drink it, drink up," Tom ordered. Amanda was the first to taste the rum.

"Oh, my gosh," she said. "This is nasty. I can't drink this!"

"You drink it or your ass is on the bus," Tom said. Elizabeth took a big gulp and spit it out. Robert sipped a little and quickly announced his dislike for the rum.

"Drink it now!" Tom yelled. They each began sipping the rum at 11:15 p.m. and did not finish until just before midnight. Amanda fell asleep at the foot of the bed and Robert ended up vomiting in the bathroom. Elizabeth was lying on a pillow against the headboard, totally passed out.

The next morning all three children were sick. They had each consumed nearly six ounces of 151° proof rum.

The rest of vacation went smoothly and they all headed back to Tennessee at the end of the week.

CHAPTER 32

Tom Rapes his Pre-Teen Sister-in-law

As they were entering the city limits back home, Tom said, "It's late, let's just let Elizabeth stay the night over here."

"It's only 9:00 o'clock, Tom, it ain't too late." Melissa responded. Tom looked at Melissa like he was daring her to say something else.

The kids were all sleeping in the back seat nestled against each other. "All right, everyone out of the car. Everybody to bed," Tom said. Amanda, Robert and Elizabeth entered the trailer one behind the other carrying their pillows and blankets. Amanda went into the bathroom and Robert and Elizabeth went straight to the bedroom. Elizabeth placed her pillow on the floor next to the bed and covered up with her blanket. Soon after, Amanda came in and climbed into bed next to Robert.

"I'm tired, too," Melissa said as she yawned and stretched out her arms. Tom told her to go to bed and said he was going to stay up for a while to have a drink and watch TV to relax a little before bed.

Close to an hour passed and Tom stood up from his recliner and removed his boots. He walked quietly into the kids' bedroom. He leaned over Elizabeth and whispered, "Get up, young lady." Elizabeth woke up somewhat disoriented, but she stood up and stumbled out of the room as Tom ordered. She walked into the living room and Tom told her to make him a drink. Elizabeth walked over to the sink and removed a glass from a plastic dish strainer. "What do you want?"

"Fix me a rum and coke," Tom ordered. Elizabeth rubbed her eyes in an attempt to clear her vision after being woken up so abruptly.

"Where is the rum?" she asked.

"Under the sink, where it always is," Tom responded, a little impatiently.

Elizabeth opened the freezer, took out an aluminum ice tray, and broke up some ice cubes for Tom's drink.

"The coke is in the ice chest," Tom said. Elizabeth poured the rum into the glass and followed with Coca-Cola from a two-liter bottle.

"Here," she said, handing Tom the glass.

Elizabeth then said, "Good night," and proceeded to return to bed.

"Come here, Elizabeth. Are you still sore at me about that thing in Daytona?" Tom asked.

"Nope, I'm just sleepy," she responded.

Tom pointed to the sofa and ordered Elizabeth to sit down.

"Come here, girl. Sit right here,"

Elizabeth was wearing white pajamas. The bottoms had a cartoon character on the right leg and the top was just a plain white button-up top with long sleeves.

Tom sat next to Elizabeth and attempted to unbutton her top. Elizabeth resisted and pulled away.

"Sit still a minute," Tom said. He reached back over and continued to unbutton her top. He took his time with each button and left the top one closed.

"Let me see what you got under here." Tom whispered.

He pulled open her pajama top and exposed Elizabeth's pale white skin. Her breasts were small with tiny pink nipples. Elizabeth sat there unable to utter a word. She knew this man would seriously hurt her if she said or did anything.

"Stand up, Elizabeth." Tom ordered.

As she stood up, Tom reached for her pajama bottoms. He tugged them slowly downwards and the bottoms began to follow his hands. After pulling the bottoms to her knees, he reached for her panties. He pulled them down very slowly, revealing that Elizabeth had already reached puberty. He pulled the panties down to her pajama bottoms and then continued pulling both to her ankles. As he attempted to remove them from under her feet, Elizabeth lost her balance and was forced to put her hand on Tom's shoulder. Tom interpreted this as a gesture of acceptance.

"Stand right here," Tom said pointing to a spot directly in front of him. Elizabeth stood there totally naked, only twelve years old.

"You're a beautiful young woman," Tom said admiringly.

"Here, unbutton my shirt for me Elizabeth."

Elizabeth reached out towards his shirt. Her hands were shaking, but she did as she was told. Tom stood up and removed his pants and underwear.

"Come here, Elizabeth," Tom whispered endearingly.

Elizabeth scooted closer to him and Tom began touching and caressing her. He was fully erect and Elizabeth didn't understand what was happening.

"I have lots of things I want to do with you tonight Elizabeth," Tom said softly into her ear.

"Let me make something clear to you first," Tom said. "What we are doing here tonight is a matter of utmost confidence. Do you believe I would hurt you, if you told somebody our secret?" Tom asked.

"Yes, sir." Elizabeth replied in a shaky and frightened voice.

"Now all you have to do is kneel down right here in front of me, Elizabeth."

CHAPTER 33

New Mini Bikes

"Hey Kids, I've got something for you," Tom said, waking up both Amanda and Robert. He told them to hurry, that it was very important.

"Get dressed and put on your jackets. It's a big surprise." Tom said with excitement. Amanda and Robert got dressed quickly and stood in the living room waiting.

"What is it? What is it?" Robert asked. Tom was as excited as they were.

"Cover your eyes!" Tom said, as he opened the door to the mobile home.

Both children walked outside, holding their hands over their eyes. Tom grabbed their hands and walked them around to the front of the trailer. He had them stand up next to each other and face in the same direction.

"Okay! Okay! Now open your eyes!" Tom exclaimed.

"Oh my God," Robert exclaimed when he saw two shiny new mini bikes, one red and one blue.

"Are those ours?" Amanda yelled with excitement.

"Yep! The red one is yours, Amanda, and the blue one belongs to you, Robert." Robert reached out to Tom hugging him.

"You are the best dad in the world," Robert said. "Ever since I was six years old I have wanted a mini bike!"

"Can we ride 'em? Can we?" Robert asked. The mini bikes were small, motorized bikes. The frames were not more than three feet off the ground. Each had a five horsepower Briggs and Stratton gasoline engine. Tom walked over to Robert's bike and bent down to open the choke. He took hold of the pull start and gave it a tug. The motor started right up on the first attempt. Robert straddled the mini and took off down to the end of the trailer park. Tom pulled on Amanda's but forgot to open the choke.

"Damn!" Tom yelled. He opened the choked and pulled again. The little motor cranked right up. "Listen to that," Tom said. "It's purring like a kitten. Hop on, Amanda."

Amanda sat on the seat and grabbed the handlebars. "All you have to do is turn this, pointing to the throttle on the handle bars. Right here, is your brake," Tom explained. Amanda turned the throttle and off she went.

Later than evening Tom, Melissa, Amanda, and Robert were sitting at the dinner table. "Everybody bow your heads for the blessing," Tom said.

"Dear Lord, we ask you to bless this meal, bless each of us and we thank you for the blessing you have bestowed on us. We thank thee for this family and the love we all have for each other. And, Lord, thank you for these beautiful children that you have blessed our lives with. Amen."

Melissa had cooked some fried chicken steak, mashed potatoes and gravy and had spent most of the day snapping beans.

"Who wants to go up into mountains tomorrow so we can ride those new dirt bikes?" Tom asked during dinner. Robert and Amanda responded simultaneously, "We do!"

The next day on the way to the mountains, the Jenkins' stopped at Kentucky Fried Chicken and bought fixens for a picnic. Both mini bikes were in the back of the truck.

CHAPTER 34

Amanda's Friend Files Rape Complaint

Mona Jones had moved to Knoxville, Tennessee in the middle of a school year. She had asked her sister Debbie if Anne could stay with her until school was out. Debbie said she would enjoy having Anne with her for a couple of months.

One night while she was staying with Debbie, Anne screamed out in the middle of the night. She was having a nightmare. Debbie ran into the room, "Oh my God, Anne, are you all right?" Anne was shaking under the covers, sobbing her heart out.

"Honey, what's wrong?" asked Debbie anxiously. "It was just a dream, Anne. It's okay now." Debbie said softly as she attempted to comfort the child.

Anne looked up sorrowfully at her aunt and sobbed, "No it's not all right, Aunt Debbie, it's real bad." She continued crying uncontrollably.

Debbie told Anne to come into the kitchen and they would fix a cup of hot chocolate and talk through the problem. Anne began telling Debbie everything that happened a year ago. "But that's not all, Aunt Debbie, he raped me, too!" Anne said with tears running down her face.

"Oh my God, honey!" Debbie said as she put her arms around Anne. Debbie picked up the phone and said, "I have to call your mom." "Please don't call right now, there ain't nothing she can do tonight, Aunt Debbie. We can call in the morning, okay?"

The next morning, Debbie called Anne's mother in Knoxville. Mona drove over immediately. She withdrew Anne from school and took her back to Knoxville with her. As soon as Mona returned, she reported the incident to the Knox County Department of Health and Human Services. Finally, she called the County District Attorney and the Sheriff's Office.

"Anne, I have made you an appointment with a therapist and tomorrow you have an appointment with a doctor," Mona told her daughter. Anne asked why she needed to see a doctor. "Honey, the doctor is a gynecologist, and she is going to take a look at you to see if you were injured during the rape."

"Anne, have you ever had sexual relations with anyone?" The doctor asked her. "No, ma'am, I haven't had sex with anyone before. I'm only 14 years old!" The doctor told her to get dressed and wait for her in the lobby. "Mrs. Jones," the doctor said. "Your daughter has been penetrated. Her hymen is no longer intact." Mrs. Jones started crying,

"That rotten son of a bitch!" she muttered under her breath.

Mona drove Anne to the Police Department and filed a police report. While she was there with Anne, Detective Shawn Crawford and Rick Vaughn took her statement. "Yes sir, Amanda's mother held me down on the bed while Mr. Jenkins had intercourse with me," she said.

"Amanda's mother told me to relax, and she helped him rape me. She is just as bad as he is! I watched her having sex with Robert and Tom had sex with Amanda. It's really gross. Robert and Amanda have sex with their Mom and stepdad all the time. She whispered as if an afterthought, "It's normal to them."

"How do you know this type of activity takes place?" Detective Vaughn asked.

"I just told you, I saw it with my own eyes and it happened to me," Anne responded. Mrs. Jones waited outside during the interview but was called in when it was over.

"All right, let's get a warrant and arrest those two bastards, right now!" Mona said with an excited but disgusted look on her face.

"Mrs. Jones. You know, I hate to tell you this, but too much time has passed since this alleged incident took place," Detective Crawford explained. "There ain't no physical evidence."

"You're putting me on," Mrs. Jones replied in disgust. "Tom Jenkins got away with raping his own daughter last year when Human Services screwed up the investigation. And this time he raped my daughter!" she exclaimed.

"Do ya'll know what happened last year, huh, do ya? She asked. "Judge Vaughn didn't force Tom Jenkins to take Amanda to an authorized doctor. Instead he let Tom, a rape and child abuse suspect, to take his victim to his own damn doctors. Not just any damn doctors, but doctors known all over the damn county to be incompetent idiots. The state had to stop their investigation and cancel a petition to seize the kids. This whole damn county is corrupt!" Mrs. Jones yelled.

Both detectives agreed to take the matter back to Health and Human Services and they asked Mona to stay out of it for the time being. The detectives reported the statement they received from Anne to Health and Human Services. An investigator was assigned to look into the matter. The multi-disciplinary team decided that, for the benefit of the children, a second inquiry was necessary.

"I think we should send an investigator back in, but if the child continues to deny the allegations, then we really need to put some closure on this case," one of the members advised.

"You realize that how we approach this child could make all the difference as to whether she cooperates and tells the truth, or whether she denies the allegations," another member added. The team agreed they needed to draft a memo to provide explicit directions to the investigator to ensure every possible stone be overturned. One of the most important requirements was to meet with the child in a location where she didn't feel threatened and to apply pressure on her without her being aware it was being done.

CHAPTER 35

Human Services Foul up

The next day, the case was assigned to Investigator Betty Gates. "Listen, before you do anything, make sure you pick up the memo in your box," the case manager emphasized to Betty. Shortly afterwards, the phone rang on Betty Gates' desk.

"Investigator Betty Gates speaking," she answered. "Oh hello, honey. No, I forgot to deposit the check, I'll run and do it right now." It was her husband. Betty jumped up and grabbed the case file on her way out, completely forgetting to pick up the memo in her box. She drove to the bank and stopped in the parking lot. She opened the case file and obtained the phone number for Amanda's school. Mrs. Gates called the school and spoke with Mr. Fletcher, the principal. He used the intercom to call Amanda's room and had her come to the office. When Amanda arrived, Mrs. Gates introduced herself and explained that she was there to follow up on the same investigation that was done last year by Mrs. Stringer. Amanda immediately became defensive and said, "Why are ya'll still doing this? I told everyone we was just lying!"

"Amanda, your friend Anne said she was raped by your stepfather last year. She said it happened after a fish fry." Mrs. Gates explained.

"Nope, that's a damn lie!" Amanda yelled. "It's all a lie."

Amanda turned away from Mrs. Gates and walked towards the door. She suddenly turned back at her and said, "Leave us alone, okay?"

She slammed the door and entered the hallway.

When Mrs. Gates reported her findings to the multi-disciplinary team, a member asked her, "Why did you call her to the principal's office? Why didn't you follow the directions in the memo?" Mrs. Gates responded by saying, "What memo?"

That evening Amanda told Tom and her mother about the investigator. "You did the right thing. We have to protect ourselves," Tom told everyone in the room. "Come here, Amanda." Tom reached around Amanda and gave her a big hug. He pulled her face up and gave her a kiss on the cheek. Then he kissed her on the lips. Amanda kissed back.

"Amanda, you know you don't have to put up with all that," Tom said. "If you want nice things and luxuries you need to get yourself a job. Listen, you don't need to keep going to school. You're fifteen years old."

"I like going to school." Amanda replied. Tom explained to Amanda that he didn't go to high school and neither did Amanda's mom, "Hell, look at us, we still got plenty of nice things." Tom told her.

"You just figure that as of today, you're a grown woman and we need to get you a job," Tom told Amanda. Melissa came over and hugged the two of them. Tom picked up Amanda and carried her to the bedroom. Both Tom and Melissa undressed Amanda on the bed. Robert was in his room doing his homework. Tom undressed Melissa and then himself. Tom told Amanda to lie down on her back. Tom and Melissa began performing oral sex on her. Robert heard the noise and knocked on their door. Tom told him to go to bed. Robert was upset and concerned about Amanda so he knocked again. Tom stood up and unlocked the door. "Come on in, son." Tom said.

CHAPTER 36

Tom Rapes his Sister-n-law Again

Tom had been in the woods all day. He was working alone and decided to call it quits at nightfall. He parked the skidder and front-end loader next to each other and drove out of the woods in the log truck. It took almost twenty minutes to get out to the road. He stopped when he reached the paved road. It was really dark that far out from town. There were no city lights, only the stars to illuminate the forest. Instead of turning to go towards his home, he drove in the direction of Ruth and Chuck's home. He knew Ruth and Chuck were at the American Legion. Tom drove the semi-truck up into the front yard and blasted the air horn. Elizabeth and her little sister Angie and brother Don came outside to greet him. "What's going on? "Where is everyone?" Tom inquired.

"Mom and Dad ain't here tonight. They went down to the American Legion Tom." Tom asked for something to drink.

"Your old man got any beer in the fridge?" Tom asked.

"Yeah, I think he's got a Budweiser or something," Elizabeth responded. Tom went into the house and washed his hands in the kitchen sink. He told Elizabeth to get him that beer.

"How old are you now, Elizabeth?" Tom yelled out.

"Thirteen."

"Shit, you're a teenager now, ain't ya?"

"Where is Melissa?" asked Elizabeth.

Tom told her he was just getting off from work and hadn't gone home yet.

"Damn, that's a cold beer!" Tom exclaimed. Elizabeth put her finger to lips, motioning for Tom keep his voice down. Her little brother Don had fallen asleep on the sofa. Tom lifted him up and took him into his room.

Elizabeth was wearing a dirty pair of blue jeans and an extra-large blue t-shirt.

Tom gave Angie five dollars and told her to go down to the store to pick him up a pack of cigarettes. She didn't want to at first but he told her to buy something for herself while she was there. Angie hopped on her bicycle and rode off. The store was eight miles round trip.

"You know, Elizabeth, in some countries 13-year-old girls are already married," Tom said. He grabbed her hand and walked her into her bedroom.

"Where are we going?" Elizabeth asked. He ordered her on to the bed.

"You lay right there," he said. He moved a rocking chair in front of the door and propped it under the door knob to prevent the door from being opened.

Elizabeth was shaking. She knew what was coming. She had been molested by him before. She pleaded with him.

"Tom, please. no, we can't. Tom, please don't do this," she said in between her tears. Tom told her to shut up.

"Why do you do this?" Tom asked. "I ain't going to hurt you,"

She wiped the tears from her eyes with a pillow case. "I'm just a little kid."

"No girl, you're a young woman, and you and me, we're going to make love." Tom stood over her and pulled her T-shirt off. He made a moaning sound and started singing, "Oh baby, baby, baby," as he removed her shirt. He ordered her to stand up and he unzipped her blue jeans. He pushed her on to the bed and lifted her up by her hips. Her jeans were very tight, and Tom was having difficulty getting them off.

"Help me here, girl." Elizabeth was unresponsive so Tom just pulled harder. He removed her jeans and panties and then sat up. He stood and removed his clothes. Elizabeth reached for a pillow and covered herself. Tom leaned over her and began kissing her mouth. She didn't kiss back. Tom began groping her breast, and then put his hand between her legs. Elizabeth knew if she resisted, he would beat the hell out of her.

Suddenly, there was a voice at the door.

"Tom! Tom!" It was Angie. She was back.

"Tom, Elizabeth!" she yelled again.

"We're in here, in Elizabeth's bedroom," Tom called back. Angie walked up to the door and attempted to open it.

"The door is locked Elizabeth, I can't get in." Angie said.

"What are ya'll doing in there? Let me in," Angie demanded.

"I can't open the stupid door," Tom called back. I'm fixing the hinges on it. Why are you back already?"

"You didn't tell me what brand of cigarettes you wanted me to buy for ya."

"Marlboro's!" Tom yelled.

"Alrighty," said Angie and she turned away and slammed the screened door on her way out. Tom turned to Elizabeth and straddled her. He made an attempt at penetration. The penetration was painful and Elizabeth cried through most of the ordeal. When Tom was finished he stood up over the bed and reminded Elizabeth what would happen to her if she told anyone.

He walked her into the bathroom and made her clean up. She was bleeding and in pain.

"I hate you!" Elizabeth sobbed.

Just as Tom was walking out the door, Ruth and Chuck drove up. They had had a couple of drinks at the Legion. Ruth got out of the car and called, "Why is Angie riding her bicycle on the road at this time of night? Where is Elizabeth!? Why are you over here, Thomas Jenkins?"

"I sent Angie to the store for me. She went to get me some cigarettes."

"Are you crazy? she is just a little girl. That's dangerous!" Ruth yelled. She yelled at Chuck and told him to get out of the car. Chuck didn't like being anywhere close to Tom, but he got out of the car and closed the door. Ruth walked into the house and

Tom followed her back inside. "Elizabeth!" she called, anxiously searching for her.

"Yes ma'am," Elizabeth answered. Elizabeth walked into the living room holding her head down. She didn't look up at her mom or Tom.

"What's the matter with you?" Ruth asked Elizabeth.

"Leave her alone," Tom said. Ruth got very mad and said,

"You mind your own business, Tom Jenkins!" Tom's face turned red with anger and he turned on to Ruth, grabbing her shirt. He raised his hand and slapped her face. Ruth fell back and stumbled, tripping over the cat sleeping on the floor. She started cursing and telling Tom how lucky he was that she didn't have a gun.

"Fuck you, old woman!" Tom yelled. He opened the door and stepped on to the front porch. Chuck was standing just outside the door with a concrete shovel raised above his head. He swung the shovel and hit Tom right in the face, cutting him just above his eye. Tom stepped back for second, and then took the shovel from Chuck. He swung the shovel against the house and broke the handle.

"You old bastard! Hit me with a damn shovel, will ya?" Tom was getting more aggravated. Chuck tried to run out the porch door but Tom grabbed him. Tom was still holding a portion of the shovel handle. He struck Chuck in the back with it several times before he decided to stop. Tom stepped up into his truck, cranked it up and drove off. He honked his air horn as he pulled away from the yard.

CHAPTER 37

Partnership Dissolution (October, 1980)

Gene Cawthorn had been after Tom for several months to dissolve their partnership. He paid an attorney to draft a partnership dissolution agreement, but he couldn't get Tom to meet with him to sign it. On October 24, 1980, they finally came together to dissolve their partnership. Tom agreed to buy Gene out and take over the entire logging operation. The agreement spelled out how the company's debts would be handled and paid by Tom Jenkins.

It listed the following outstanding debts.

Valco Company	$1,700.00
Branchwater Bank	$11,000.00 payable @ $272.26 per month
Transnorth Financial Services	$17,998.00 payable @ $329.00 per month

Secured by the title to residence of Gene and Margaret Cawthorn

Branchwater Valley Bank	$21,100.00

Co-signed by Tom Hines

In addition to assuming responsibility for the company debts, Tom agreed to pay Gene Cawthorn $3,800.00.

The agreement made it very clear that Tom could not sell or dispose of any of the equipment until the debts were paid in full. The agreement gave Gene the right to re-possess any or all the equipment in the event of non-payment.

Tom and Gene shook hands after signing the dissolution. Tom commented, "Hell, this is like getting a damn divorce, ain't it?"

"Yeah, I reckon," Gene replied. Once on the sidewalk they turned and walked in separate directions. Gene and his wife Margaret sat down in their car and Margaret shook her head.

"I just don't trust him, Gene. My Daddy's standing out there on a limb for this man. If he don't pay up, Daddy has to pay off that second loan to the bank."

"What about us Margaret? We'd have to pay the first one and we don't have it."

Three months passed by and the banks started sending default letters to Gene and his father-in-law Tom Hines.

CHAPTER 38

Tom and Melissa Skip Town

Gene called Tom's house and the phone was answered by a phone company recording, "The number you are calling has been disconnected." Gene hung up and immediately drove to Tom's trailer, only to discover it was vacant. Gene screamed in frustration.

"Damn it! That son of a bitch!" He jumped into his pickup truck, cranked it up and put the accelerator to the floor. Rocks and debris kicked up on to the trailer as he sped off. Gene drove to the Roberts' house and asked Ruth where Tom and Melissa were. Her response wasn't what he wanted to hear.

"I think they done up and moved to Florida. They went somewhere down there, not sure exactly where. I just feel sorry for those two young 'uns," Ruth complained.

Margaret went to the school and managed to track down Melissa Jenkins through the school transfer papers.

They were living in a small town in Central Florida called Lake Alfred.

Margaret called the number she had obtained from the school, and Melissa answered the phone, "Hello."

"Melissa!"

Margaret said, "This is Margaret Cawthorn. What are you doing in Florida? Ya'll just took off and didn't say nothing to nobody and you ain't paying the bills! You left us in a hell of mess up here up with the banks and the IRS." Margaret said.

"You know what? Tom is on easy street now and we got it made. To tell you the truth we don't want nutt'n else to do with you or anybody else in Tennessee."

"Why, you sorry bitch!" Margaret screamed down the phone, as Melissa hung up on her.

That evening Gene came home and he and Margaret agreed to hire an auditor to research where the money was.

The auditor concluded Tom hadn't made any payments on any of the bank loans in months. He discovered Melissa had been paying their personal electric bills, car payments, medical bills and insurance payments with company funds. To make matters worse, she had even been buying groceries out of the company checking account.

Just prior to their departure, Tom sold a company truck to a car dealer. He used the money to make a down payment on a new car. It was later determined that Tom had forged Gene Cawthorn's name on the paper work in order to purchase the car.

Gene and Margaret, along with Margaret's father, Thomas Hines filed a police report with the County sheriff's office, alleging that Tom Jenkins stole their money and that he intentionally cheated and deprived Thomas Hines of his money.

As it turned out, Gene Cawthorn and his wife got divorced. The bank filed a lien against their home. Thomas Hines, who had retired at age seventy, was forced to pay the co-signed loan with his social security income.

The sheriff turned the case over the District Attorney who decided to give it to the Grand Jury.

The Grand Jury heard the case in February of 1981 and issued a **TRUE BILL**. That meant they had found sufficient evidence to support that:

> *Tom Jenkins and Melissa Jenkins did unlawfully, fraudulently, and feloniously appropriate to their own use certain personal property of Mr. Thomas Hines, to wit: by receiving $20,277.60 from Mr. Hines with a promise to re-pay and thereafter failing to re-pay said money with the intent to cheat, deprive, and defraud Mr. Thomas Hines.*

Unfortunately Tom and Melissa Jenkins were longer in the state of Tennessee. The enforcement of the Grand Jury investigation could only continue if the Jenkins were in Tennessee.

CHAPTER 39

Final Investigation in Tennessee

The rape crisis center in Knoxville, Tennessee notified the local office of Health and Human Services in February 1981 that they were counseling a young lady, Anne Jones, who had alleged she was raped by Tom Jenkins. During therapy sessions, Anne Jones, now fourteen years of age, mentioned that Elizabeth Roberts, Charles Thomas Jenkins's sister-n-law in Athens, had also been raped by Tom Jenkins.

The investigation was assigned to Health and Human Services Investigator J. B. Pearce. Mrs. Pearce visited the high school and met with Elizabeth Roberts. The two met in the principal's office.

"Elizabeth, my name is Mrs. Pearce and I work with Health and Human Services. I need to talk to you about some things that are going to be very personal"

"What is that you want? I haven't done anything wrong," said Elizabeth.

Mrs. Pearce explained to Elizabeth she had been informed that Elizabeth may have been sexually abused by Tom Jenkins. As soon as Mrs. Pearce made that statement, Elizabeth started shaking and became very nervous. "Were you raped by this man?" Mrs. Pearce asked.

Elizabeth explained that Tom Jenkins was her sister's husband. Mrs. Pearce explained to Elizabeth that she was familiar with who he was.

"Did he rape you?" she again asked.

Elizabeth's looked down in shame. Tears dropped from her eyes on to her pants. Mrs. Pearce handed her a tissue. Elizabeth looked up at her and responded.

"Yes, ma'am, he sure did."

Mrs. Pearce asked Elizabeth to explain to her when and where these rapes occurred. Elizabeth explained the first time she was raped she was sleeping over at her sister's home after a trip to Florida. She said everyone was sleeping and Tom woke her up and made her prepare him a drink. "After I fixed him the drink, he made me take off all of my clothes and then raped me on the sofa."

"Where was Melissa while this was happening?"

"She was sleeping."

"What did you do afterwards, Elizabeth? Did you tell anyone?"

"I didn't do nutt'n. I didn't tell nobody because Tom told me he would kill me if I ever said anything to anyone, and he would, you know. And he still will, Mrs. Pearce!" Elizabeth said sobbing.

Mrs. Pearce asked her, "Was that the only time he raped you?"

"No ma'am, altogether he raped me four or five times. One time he came over to our house and sent my little sister to the store. My little brother was sleeping. He raped me in my bedroom. My door was missing the lock so he blocked the door with a piece of furniture."

Mrs. Pearce shook her head in disbelief and asked Elizabeth when these rapes happened. Elizabeth said she wasn't sure of the exact date, but she knew one happened after their vacation to Daytona and the last one was within the last year. "I haven't seen him or any of them since that time. Mrs. Pearce, do you know that Tom beats up on my sister and on Amanda and Robert?" Elizabeth explained that Amanda regularly had sex with Tom. "The first time he raped me I was only thirteen years old!" Elizabeth cried.

Mrs. Pearce told Elizabeth she would need to sit with her mother and dad to discuss these incidents. Elizabeth said she understood.

On February 10, 1981, Mrs. Pearce called Ruth Roberts and asked her to come to Health and Human Services office. She told her there was a serious problem involving Elizabeth. Two days passed and she didn't hear a word from the Roberts'. Mrs. Pearce drove to the Roberts home and when seated in their living room, asked Ruth why she didn't come immediately to the office when she was told of the accusations. Ruth responded, "I don't know. I just don't rightly know."

Chuck was sitting next to Ruth while Mrs. Pearce was explaining how Elizabeth was raped by Tom Jenkins. Ruth sat there and didn't say a word. It was as if she didn't hear what Mrs. Pearce was saying. Chuck rolled a Prince Albert cigarette as he sat there. Some of the tobacco fell on to the floor. He lifted the poorly wrapped cigarette to his lips and wet it. Afterwards he twisted and rolled it into a cigarette. He shook his head in disgust, "I figured something wasn't right. You know, he broke my wife's wrist one time. He's caused us all sorts of problems throughout all these years." Chuck said. "I probably won't ever see my daughter again. She sure was a cute baby when she was born." Chuck reminisced. Chuck handed Mrs. Pearce a baby photo of Melissa that was on the end table next to the sofa.

"Yes, sir, she was a cute baby, Mrs. Pearce concurred.

Mrs. Pearce explained she wanted to arrange therapy for Elizabeth.

"Heck, I don't know. I don't reckon we could afford that," Chuck responded anxiously. Mrs. Pearce shook her head and with a smile told Chuck that the therapy would be provided by the state at cost to him and his wife.

"Mr. Roberts, we need to do something right away. 'Cause if we don't, Elizabeth just may have some terrible problems when she becomes an adult." Mrs. Pearce explained.

Ruth and Chuck agreed, but said they couldn't afford to pay anybody.

On February 21, 1981, Mrs. Pearce picked up Elizabeth from school and drove her to the district attorney's office. Anne Jones and her mother Mona were there. Anne had already provided a statement. Elizabeth sat through an intense interview with an assistant district attorney and explained everything she could remember.

After the interview, Mona took Elizabeth home with her and Anne to Knoxville. Both children played together for the weekend and according to Mona it was good therapy for both of them.

The assistant District Attorney contacted Mrs. Pearce in March and asked her meet with him. She drove down to the District attorney's office and after waiting for almost an hour in the lobby the receptionist told her he was available. The receptionist buzzed her through the door and escorted her to a conference room. The attorney came in and sat down, bringing a case file with him.

Mrs. Pearce, you know we probably have enough evidence here to bring this case before the Grand Jury. The testimony of Jenkins' victims might just get us a conviction. I also want to say that you did a very good job running this down.

"But ….?" said Mrs. Pearce knew there was a "but" coming.

"Well, Tom Jenkins isn't even living in this county any more. Hell, he isn't even living in this state. I'll be honest with you, if he was still in Tennessee we would be vigorously pursuing this man and prosecution of this case, but due to the circumstances, we've decided not to continue. We're going to drop it."

Mrs. Pearce was extremely upset to hear this, considering all the coaching she had had to do get Elizabeth to endure all those embarrassing interviews.

After learning the state was dropping the case, Mrs. Pearce maintained monthly contact with Elizabeth and her parents. By the end of the year, Elizabeth had missed more school than she had attended. Mrs. Pearce continued doing what she could to keep her in school and therapy.

NOTE:

In February 1981, Tom and Melissa loaded up a U-Haul truck, packed up Amanda and Robert, and in the middle of the night, quietly slipped out of their home town in Southern Tennessee.

They moved to a small town in Polk County, Florida called Lake Alfred. Robert and Amanda were both registered into school on February 20, into the Polk County School system. The school records indicated they were both withdrawn on March 29. A handwritten notation on Robert's record stated he was being withdrawn because he and his family were moving back to Tennessee. We later learned that Tom was pissed off because Margaret had located them. Without any discussion, he told everyone on March 29, that they were leaving. They actually moved to somewhere in Georgia. The exact location in Georgia is unknown. Neither Amanda nor Robert attended school again until they moved to Florida four months later. Tom enrolled Robert into a Middle School, but he convinced Amanda that school was a waste of time. He explained to Amanda that if she wanted the luxuries in life she would need to get a job. Tom bought Amanda a used Corvette on her 16th birthday and somewhere around this time, is where the story continues,

CHAPTER 40

Amanda has a Boyfriend

Amanda had just started a new job at a local restaurant located on main highway on the west side of town. She was seventeen years old. She stood looking at herself in the mirror. She put on a dark shade of lipstick, mascara and blush on her freckled cheeks. She liked what she saw and was thankful that she grown up to become an attractive young woman. She put away her makeup and picked up a washcloth and wiped all the make-up from her face. She knew Tom would never permit her to leave the house with make-up on her face.

As she was leaving for work, Tom called her into the kitchen. He was sitting with Melissa and Robert.

"What time are you supposed to be there this evening?" he asked. Amanda replied her shift started at 8:00 p.m. Tom told her he wanted to see her schedule.

"Tom, it's Friday night and someone is always scheduled for 8 o'clock," Amanda explained.

He demanded to see her schedule, so she went into her bedroom and brought it back out for him.

"You see," said Amanda triumphantly.

"All right, you get off at 3:00 a.m. You bess be home no later than 3:15 a.m. Do you understand me?" Tom warned. Amanda replied with, "Yes, sir."

She reached over and kissed Tom on his forehead and told him good bye. "Bye, Mom," she called as she walked out the front door.

When she got to work she realized she had left her name tag at home. Her boss asked "Where's your name tag, Amanda?"

"It broke!" Amanda lied. Her boss responded in disbelief.

"It broke, huh? Why didn't you bring in the broken pieces?"

Amanda had been reporting for work late since she started and her boss was beginning to doubt her. "All right, you are the hostess tonight," she said. Amanda looked up at her and said, "Okay, that's cool."

Being hostess was not too bad of a position to be working on a Friday night. All the drunks would come in after the bars closed. The waitress had the toughest job. Six hours had passed and it had been relatively quiet. The bars in town were closing and the restaurant parking lot had gone from having a couple of cars to almost full in a matter of minutes. Amanda greeted a party of four young white males.

"Hi welcome to Denny's, do you want smoking or non-smoking?"

One of the men looked at Amanda and said, "I want to smoke you baby."

He looked back at his friends and the four of them laughed. Another member of the group apologized for his behavior and said, "He's just drunk, we'll take smoking please."

Amanda escorted them to a booth and as the group took their seats the young man who had just apologized looked at Amanda. Their eyes were locked for brief moment. Amanda had a strange feeling inside. "He's cute," she thought to herself. The group all ordered Grand Slams and coffee and were on their way out the door in less than forty-five minutes.

The young man came back inside the restaurant and stuck out his hand to introduce himself to Amanda. "My name is Rod," he said with a broad smile. Amanda wasn't sure how to respond so she shook his hand and told him she was pleased to meet him. He asked her what her name was and she pointed to her name tag, but then realized it wasn't there.

"Amanda, my name is Amanda," she blurted out. Rod asked, "Can I call you sometime?" She instinctively replied, "No! I mean yeah, sure, but when, she didn't have a phone.

"You'll have to come by here she told him." Amanda knew Tom would never allow a boy to call her at home. Rod left, and for the first time in her life Amanda was experiencing normal adolescent feelings of excitement for the opposite sex. Her body was tingling. She actually felt good. The next night, Rod returned and sat with Amanda during her break. They hit it off really good.

"Let's go out or something, when are you off?"

Amanda knew she wouldn't be able to date him on her nights off so she said she was free Sunday night. He asked for her address, but she refused to give out. She told him to meet her at the 7-11 down the street at 6:00 p.m.

Rod was three years her senior. He was a tall, handsome young man, 5'11" tall with dark curly hair. He had recently moved to Florida from a small town in southern Indiana. He worked in Construction as a laborer.

He and Amanda met the next night. Amanda called in sick and didn't go to work. As far as Tom knew, she was working. She parked her car behind Denny's and they drove off in Rod's Chevy Malibu. "I have to be home no later than 12:15 a.m." She explained to Rod.

"Why is that? Do you turn into a pumpkin after midnight?" He laughed. Amanda chuckled and responded, "Something like that."

Rod took Amanda to a Mexican restaurant for dinner in Orlando. He treated her like queen. As Amanda was being seated in the restaurant, Rod stood behind her and pulled her chair out, "Thank you!" Amanda told him, feeling very proud to be with such a gentleman. Rod replied, "You're very welcome and you're very beautiful."

When they left the restaurant, Rod opened Amanda's car door and closed it behind her. Amanda felt like she had died and gone to heaven. Afterwards, Rod drove to Orlando International Airport and parked his car on a road directly underneath the approach to the North-South runway.

Within minutes, their bodies were entwined and their lips were all over each other's faces. Rod began stroking and gently caressing Amanda's breast. Amanda was becoming excited. She was sixteen years old and for the first time in her life she was experiencing feelings of sexual desire. This is what normal people feel, she thought. Their kisses were passionate and their breathing was heavy and rapid. Rod unbuttoned Amanda's blouse and placed his fingers between her bra and breast. His fingers pinched at her nipples. Amanda was moaning and enjoying every minute of this normal relationship. Rod unlatched Amanda's bra and exposed her breasts. They weren't very large, but the fact they were exposed and she didn't resist, made him equally excited. Their lips seemed permanently connected until Rod moved towards Amanda's breast. Within minutes, both Amanda and Rod were totally naked in the car. They moved to the back seat. They made love that evening, but only after nearly an hour of passionate kissing and warm loving embraces. Rod took Amanda back to her car and they made arrangements to see each other again.

When Amanda got home Tom was still awake. He was sitting on the sofa watching television. He was wearing a white hotel robe. Amanda immediately felt a cold chill run down her spine. She knew Tom was awake for one reason. He wanted to have sex. Rod didn't use a condom and he had ejaculated into her vagina. She had no fear of pregnancy because Tom had put her on the pill when she was ten or eleven years old.

"Come here, Amanda," Tom ordered.

"Just a minute Dad, I need to pee first, okay?" She went into the bathroom and removed a douche bottle from underneath the sink. She kept repeating to herself, "Oh my God, Oh my God, I'm dead!" She douched several times trying to cleanse the sperm and vaginal fluids from her vagina. Afterwards she dried herself the best she could.

She walked back apprehensively and said, "Okay, phew, I feel better now."

"Come here baby. Come over here and sit next to me," said Tom affectionately.

Amanda walked over and sat next to Tom and asked, "What are you watching on TV? Where's Mom? Is she in bed?"

Tom put his arm around Amanda and whispered in her ear. "I love you baby." Amanda could smell alcohol on his breath. Tom continued. "You are a better wife to me than your mother." Amanda shuddered and told him that she was not his wife, but his daughter. Tom replied, "Not by blood."

He began unbuttoning Amanda's top, then he removed her bra. "Take off your pants, honey," Tom said. Amanda removed her pants first, then her panties. Tom moved his head in between Amanda's bare legs. He paused and began inhaling. Amanda's heart skipped a beat. She knew he had detected something. "He knows," she thought. She immediately pulled at Tom's robe to remove him from her vaginal area. She untied the robe and Tom was naked underneath. His penis was erect. Amanda reached for him, "Lay down on the sofa Dad." Tom interrupted her and said,

"Don't call me Dad when we are making love. Call me Tom." he ordered.

"Okay Tom." Amanda replied.

"Lay down on your back."

Tom laid back on the sofa as Amanda performed oral sex on him. After climaxing, Tom fell asleep on the sofa. Amanda covered him with a blanket and went to bed. She fell asleep thinking about Rod. "I think I am in love," she thought to herself. She had a big smile on her face as she drifted off to sleep.

Amanda and Rod had been dating for several months before she showed him where she lived. She told him her stepdad was very abusive, crazy and very mean. They made arrangements to meet one morning and spend the entire day with each other. Amanda planned to call in sick at work that day. She was scheduled for an early morning shift. She told her girlfriend she thought she was in love with Rod.

The day arrived. It was a muggy and damp Central Florida morning. The grass was saturated with early morning dew and there were pockets of heavy fog throughout most of the community. Tom had left for work and Melissa was on her way to Robert's school. Amanda called her boss at Denny's and said she was sick. She drove her 1984 Z-28 to Rod's house. Rod's parents were home and Amanda was invited in to wait for him. Mrs. Stevens asked Amanda what their plans were for the day. "I don't know. Maybe we'll see a matinee at the theater and then we might go for a walk along the lake front," Amanda replied. Rod came out of his room and gave Amanda a quick kiss and grabbed her hand. It was obvious that love was blossoming. "I need to drop back by the house." Amanda told Rod as they got into her car. She parked outside her apartment and told Rod to wait there. She explained she needed to change her work schedule since Tom would look at it. She didn't want him getting suspicious and spoiling their day. Just as Amanda entered the apartment, Tom drove into the parking lot and saw Rod sitting in her car. He parked his truck behind a moving van and waited. Tom got out of his truck and shut the door quietly. He opened his bed-mounted tool box and removed a claw hammer. He heard Amanda closing the apartment door and cautiously moved a little closer, making sure she didn't see him. Amanda yelled out to Rod, "I need Tom to think I'm off and visiting a girlfriend in case he comes home before we get back. "If not, he will call Denny's and I will be in big trouble."

They were sitting in Amanda's car with the windows closed and air conditioning on as Amanda further explained her plan. Rod scooted Amanda towards him and the two embraced. Suddenly there was a deafening crash. The passenger window exploded and glass particles sprayed all over Rod and Amanda.

"You damn son of bitch!" Tom yelled, as he grabbed Rod's hair. He pulled him through the open window. "I'll kill you, you bastard."

Rod was screaming and resisting the best he could, but Tom was much stronger. Amanda screamed for Tom to stop. "Leave him alone, stop it. I love him Tom, stop it!"

Tom dragged Rod almost fifty feet to Tom's truck and violently slammed Rod's head against the front bumper. Rod squealed in pain, begging Tom to stop.

"I'll stop. I'll stop when you're dead, you son of bitch! You'd better never be in one of my cars again! You stay the fuck away from my property!" Tom had a small sheath on his belt where he kept a large folding knife. He removed the knife from its holster and began threatening to kill Rod. "I'll cut your fucking throat!" he screamed, as he placed the knife against Rod's neck. Tom's face was beet-red with anger and Rod was sure Tom was going to kill him. Amanda could see Tom was way out of control. She knew there was no way to stop him. "He's going to kill my boyfriend," she thought.

She was pretty certain that if she jumped out of the car and started running away, Tom would stop attacking Rod to pursue her. Amanda slammed the car door and yelled out, "No!"

She took off running and heard Tom scream, "Amanda! Dam it!"

She ran as fast as she could but heard Tom's heavy footsteps gaining on her, so she stopped and turned towards him. She thought, "I'm just going to have to face up to it." Tom, panting and gasping for air, approached Amanda and grabbed her by her hair. He lifted her upwards, forcing her to walk on her tiptoes. "You been fucking, haven't you?" Tom yelled.

"You been fucking that boy, you slutty fucking whore!"

Amanda was trembling with fear as she responded, "Yeah! Yes Tom, I have fucked him but only one time, I swear!"

With one hand still holding on to Amanda's hair, Tom struck her in the face with his spare hand. His knuckles ripped through her bottom lip. Amanda's blood splattered over Tom's face and his white work shirt. Amanda began crying hysterically.

"Where does that son of bitch live? Take me to his damn house right fucking now."

He handed Amanda an orange shop rag to wipe her face off and ordered her into the truck.

Amanda directed Tom to Rod's parent home and Tom told Amanda to get out and come with him. Tom pounded on the door with his fist. Mrs. Stevens opened the door and, wide-eyed, asked what on earth was wrong.

"Where is that damn piece-of-shit son of yours?" Tom yelled.

"I beg your pardon!" Mrs. Stevens was in shock.

Tom asked her again where her son was. "I thought he was with Amanda," Mrs. Stevens said. Just then, Rod walked up, blood dripping from a gash above his left eye. Tom pulled his knife from its sheath and started running at Rod, "I'll kill you, you son of bitch."

Amanda just stood there screaming. Mrs. Stevens threatened to call the police.

"Don't you ever come near my daughter again! You understand me, boy? I will cut your fucking nuts off!" Tom yelled.

He turned to Amanda, "You get back in my fucking truck!"

Amanda sat in the truck up against the door crying during the entire drive home. "You stay the fuck away from that boy unless you want me to fucking gut that bastard and throw him in a damn swamp for the alligators to eat! Do you hear me?" Tom ranted.

He pushed her head against the truck window and whispered, "I give you everything you need Amanda. You have a new car, nice clothes, good sex and everything else you need. Why did you do this to me?"

CHAPTER 41

Robert's Report Card and Suicide Attempt

Robert was attending a different middle school and was in the seventh grade. His transition to Florida schools had been very difficult for him. He had missed almost half his first year in 1981. He had been in trouble a dozen times for fighting and his grades were barely passing. He was standing in the hallway talking to a friend when the bell rang. "I'm in real bad trouble," Robert confided to his friend.

"My Dad is going to kill me when he sees my report card."

His friend suggested he just hide it or only have his Mom sign it. Robert shook his head, "You don't know my Dad.

I have to show him the report card, or it will be much worse."

Robert walked dejectedly into his homeroom class and the teacher began to call roll. As each student answered, she handed them their report card. The dreaded moment came and the teacher called Robert's name. "Here!" Robert replied.

The teacher told him to come up to her desk and pick up his card. Robert walked towards her with his head down. He had been sweating all week in anticipation of what his grades were going to be. He walked back to his seat and when the bell rang Robert didn't move. His homeroom teacher had to tell him he could leave.

His Mom picked him up after school and took him home. "What's wrong with you?" Melissa asked. "Nothing," Robert solemnly replied.

Melissa dropped Robert off at the apartment and left.

Robert walked into his bedroom and sat on his bed. His entire body was shaking with fear. "God, please take me right now, take me away. Don't make me live through this."

Tears began to run down his face, as he contemplated his miserable fate.

"I guess I have to do it, since you won't. I don't believe you are real anyhow. If you was, you wouldn't let this shit happen to us," Robert thought as he walked into the bathroom and slowly opened the medicine cabinet.

His intention was to take a bunch of his mother's valium, but he stumbled on to a box of straight razors. He removed the box from the cabinet and just held it in his hand. He put the toilet seat cover down, and sat on it. He started crying as he opened the box of razors. He removed a single straight razor, and unwrapped the protective cover. "I know I have to cut long ways," he contemplated.

He pressed the razor blade into his pale, fragile wrist. "I'll cut sideways," he thought.

He slowly began moving the razor from one side of his wrist to the other. Blood began to ooze, little by little, from the newly-created laceration. He cut a tiny, thin line across his wrist. It was not deep enough to cause lethal bleeding.

After dropping off Robert at home, Melissa drove up to the takeout window at Hardee's restaurant, where Amanda was working as a cashier.

"May I take your order please?" Amanda asked over the intercom.

"Hey, honey, it's Mom."

"Hey, Mom."

"Your brother is acting very strange today. I think you need to check on him."

Yes ma'am. I get off in ten minutes. I'll go straight home."

Meanwhile, Robert continued to work on a way to avoid the impending confrontation with his stepdad.

"I have to do this!" Robert said out loud, as he winced in pain and pushed the blade deeper into his skin.

The pain was too intense, so he stopped. He watched the blood slowly trickle down from his wrist on to the toilet seat. Robert picked the razor and again pressed the edge into his skin. He didn't place it along the same cut, because it hurt too much. As he pressed the razor deeper into his skin, the blood began dripping at a faster pace from his wrist.

At this point, Amanda entered the front door and called him, "Robert, Robert!"

She burst open the bathroom door and screamed when she saw the blood, "Robert, what are you doing?"

Robert dropped the razor onto the floor and put his head into his lap.

"Amanda, leave me alone. I have to do this!" His voice was muffled and faint.

"No, you don't, Robert. Why?"

Robert looked up at her, his eyes red and swollen from crying.

"I have two F's on my report card. You remember what happened last time. Dad is going to kill me, so let me die my way."

"No! No! Damn it!" You are not going to die, I told you one day all this shit will be over, Robert!"

"How? What are we going to do? Kill him first?" Robert was distraught and had totally given up.

Amanda sat on the bathroom floor, looking lovingly up at Robert.

"Maybe. Why not? We could do it. We just have to make it look like self-defense that's all."

Robert looked at Amanda like she was crazy, "How would we do it?" he asked, hoping she was telling the truth.

136

"We'll shoot him, that's what we'll do!" Amanda exclaimed.

Robert laughed at the thought. "We don't even have a gun," he said.

"Let's get this mess cleaned up before Tom gets home. Don't show him your report card. I'll sign it for you." Amanda said.

"Let's go over to Kelly's house and watch some TV." Amanda whispered.

"How am I going to explain these cuts to Dad?" Robert asked.

"Hell I don't know. Wear a long-sleeved shirt. If he sees your wrist, tell him you tried to kill yourself but changed your mind."

When Amanda cranked up her Z-28 she accelerated several times creating a small cloud of smoke behind the car. She put it in drive and left rubber marks on the pavement. They drove through town to a large subdivision near the county line where her friend Kelly lived.

They were sitting in Kelly's house watching "An Officer and a Gentleman" starring Richard Gere and Debra Winger. In the last scene, Richard Gere walks into a factory and lifts up his girlfriend and carries her away. Amanda was teary-eyed and Robert made fun of her. Amanda suddenly realized the time.

"Oh shit. It's 10 o'clock. We're dead meat! Let's go!" Amanda yelled." Amanda and Robert jumped into the car and sped off.

On the way home, Amanda laid out to Robert her master plan as to what they should tell Tom.

"Okay, Robert. Let's get our stories straight. We were watching the movie and lost track of time, right? As soon as we realized what time it was, we rushed home. Okay, don't change it!"

As they pulled into the parking lot, Tom was standing outside the front door. Their hearts sank.

"Oh shit! Robert, you go straight past him and I will deal with him." Amanda said protectively. Amanda walked up to Tom with Robert behind her.

"What's up Dad?"

"Where the fuck have you been? Do you know what time it is?" "Yes, sir!" Amanda replied.

Robert slipped past Tom and went inside. Melissa was sleeping on the sofa. Next to her on the side table, was a bottle of valium and a glass of water.

Tom ordered Amanda inside and said, "I know what you've been doing. You've been out fucking," he yelled.

"No sir. We was at Kelly's house in BVL," Amanda replied.

Tom grabbed Amanda by the hand and led her into the bathroom. "Pull down your pants!" He ordered.

Amanda unbuckled her belt and zipped down her pants.

"Take them off!"

Amanda pulled her pants down and stepped out of them. She left her panties on.

"Everything!" Tom said.

She took off her panties and tossed them on the sink. Tom ordered her to put down the toilet seat and sit down.

"Spread your legs. I told you I was going to inspect you from now on, didn't I?"

Amanda looked at him innocently. "Yes sir, but I didn't do anything." Tom inserted his finger into Amanda's vagina to see if she was wet. "Okay, you passed the test. Now get dressed."

Tom walked out of the bathroom, picked up Melissa from the sofa and carried her to bed.

He went into the kitchen and made himself a drink then entered the living room. He sat down and called Robert and Amanda to come in there with him. They walked in and sat down next to each other.

"Where the fuck were you two tonight? And don't lie to me." Tom demanded.

Robert responded first. "We was at Kelly's house watching An Officer and a Gentleman."

"That's right!" Amanda said.

Tom had a glass in his hand about half-full of Jack Daniels whiskey. He took a sip and turned towards Robert.

"Tell me the truth, boy!"

Tom slammed his drink on to the coffee table. Robert and Amanda both said in tandem, "We were at Kelly's house."

Tom got up from his recliner and walked into the kitchen.

"Call Kelly, if you don't believe us!"

Amanda was terrified at the thought of what Tom's next move might be.

Tom opened a utility drawer and removed a pair of pliers. He walked back into the living room and sat down. He drank the last half of his drink and belched out loud. Amanda and Robert sat there staring at him. Tom stood and walked up to Robert. He took the pliers and squeezed them shut on to a lock of Robert's hair.

"You fucking liar! He jerked his hand and pliers away from Robert's head. Robert shrieked out in pain.

"You motherfucker!" Robert blurted out. Tom took the back of his hand and slapped Robert's face. Amanda sat there quietly.

"You called me a motherfucker! I'll kill you, you little fucking bastard! I'm your damn father!" Tom was beet-red and out of control once again.

Robert became defiant, "You ain't my dad. My dad lives in Tennessee."

"Yeah, right, the Dad who loved you so much he gave you up for adoption. You can pack up your shit tonight and go back to that cocksucker!" Tom snarled.

He pushed Robert on to the floor and straddled him. Robert attempted to push him off, and in the process managed to expose his wrist cuts. Tom grabbed his wrist and yelled. "What the fuck is this? What did you do? You are one fucked-up kid. What did you do, try to kill yourself? You want to die?"

Tom began strangling Robert. Amanda jumped on to Tom's back and tried to pull him off. She pulled his hair and bit him on the shoulder. Tom balled up his fist and struck Amanda in her jaw. She dropped on to the floor and laid there unconscious.

Robert yelled, "You killed her!"

Tom interrupted his assault on Robert to turn his attention to Amanda. He lifted her head up to his knees and shook her in an attempt to wake her. Tom opened her eyelids and saw that her pupils were rolled back. He shook her again and she came to.

"Go to bed Robert!' He put the pliers down on the carpet. A clump of Robert's hair was still attached.

The next morning Robert didn't go to school and Amanda didn't go to work. As a matter of fact, Robert missed the next three days and Amanda was fired from Hardee's for being a no-call and no-show.

CHAPTER 42

The Last Straw

Robert was in his bedroom watching television and Amanda had just returned from Burger King. She was munching on a chicken sandwich. The front door opened. It was Tom. "Hey, I'm home," he announced.

Amanda had eaten half the sandwich and was about to eat the rest, when she heard Tom say, "Let's go out to dinner!"

"Oh my God!" Amanda thought. She knew Tom would explode if he knew she had eaten already.

"Let's go out to eat." Tom said again. She quickly wrapped up the sandwich and put it into the garbage can. Melissa said she was hungry.

"Me, too!" Amanda and Robert said in unison.

Tom had a beer can in his hand and was headed for the trash can to discard it. He popped open the lid and dropped the can inside and just stood there. He looked around the room and noticed Amanda was very nervous. Tom scratched his head, and then re-opened the trash can. He reached in and removed the sandwich.

"Is this your sandwich, Amanda?" Tom asked accusingly. Amanda responded with a shaky, "Yes sir, it's mine, but I didn't eat it all."

"Damn it!" Tom yelled. He walked over to Amanda and threw the sandwich in her face. The mayonnaise and lettuce stuck to her hair.

"Every fucking time I want this family to eat together, you go and fuck it up!" He screamed. Out of the blue, Tom swung and backhanded Amanda in the face. Robert yelled for him to stop and Tom grabbed Robert by his throat and told him to shut his fucking mouth. At that point Robert walked out of the kitchen.

"Why is it that nobody in this family gets it? You know damn well we are going to eat at night and we always eat together.

Why can't you have enough respect for your family to not go out and buy a damn hamburger before we eat?"

Tom was screaming at the top of his lungs. "You just get the fuck out of my house and don't fucking come back!" Tom yelled.

Amanda looked at Tom and said, "I think Mom has something to tell you about the insurance!" Melissa looked at Amanda and asked, "Why did you say that?" Melissa looked at Tom and began apologizing.

"I'm sorry, Tom I swear I didn't mean to."

"Mean to what?"

"Well, I got a notice in the mail yesterday that if I didn't pay the insurance it was going to be cancelled. I didn't want you to be mad at me, so I paid the insurance from the Sun bank account. Then I went to NCNB and got me a cash advance on the Visa card. I took that money and put it back in the Sun Bank account. I didn't want you to get mad at me."

Tom stared at Melissa for a minute, then bent over and picked up a five pound dumbbell from the floor and threw it at her. It missed Melissa by a few inches and struck the sofa. Melissa fell back and her right arm went between the sofa cushions and the left arm of the sofa. The springs tore into her skin, causing a laceration the length of her forearm. Melissa yelped in pain. Tom walked over to her menacingly.

"You fucking liar. After all these years, I still can't trust you!" He grabbed Melissa's hair and pulled her to the floor. Melissa relaxed her body and lay motionless on the floor. Tom became even more aggravated and kicked her in the stomach yelling, "You and your fucking daughter can get the fuck out of my house!"

Melissa stood up, but she couldn't stand straight due to the pain in her stomach. Amanda grabbed her mother's hand and said, "Come on Mom."

Melissa picked up her purse and they headed for the door. Tom yelled for them to stop. You ain't going nowhere with my money and credit cards. Take them out right now and put them right here," he pointed to the coffee table. Melissa turned her purse upside down and dumped the entire contents on the coffee table. Then she just dropped her purse. Her arm was still bleeding. Amanda grabbed her hand again and motioned for her to leave.

They walked outside and Melissa told Amanda she had a friend at work called Ann who was leaving to New York tomorrow. She told Amanda that she thought maybe they could ride with her and get away from here. "She just lives around the corner." Melissa said.

"Mom, your arm is bleeding pretty badly. I'll put something on it at Ann's house." She replied.

Melissa and Amanda walked up to the door and before Melissa had a chance to knock, Tom drove up in his truck. He yelled out of the passenger window for them to get into the truck.

"Maybe he's over it," Melissa said to Amanda. "Come on let's go."

Melissa jumped into the truck and scooted next to Tom. Amanda sat next to the door. Tom backed up on Ann's grass and turned around. He accelerated the truck, causing the tires to spin out digging a rut in her yard. He drove past the street that would have taken them home.

"Where are we going?" Amanda asked anxiously.

"I am just tired of the two of you liars. You don't have any respect for our money. I have been thinking about this for a long time and I think the timing is right now."

"What? What is right?" Melissa's body shook with fear." Tom looked at Melissa and with a stone-cold face replied, "I am going to kill ya both. Right fucking tonight! This is your last day on this earth."

Melissa started crying and yelling at him to stop saying that. Amanda opened the truck door with the intention of jumping out, but Tom was going too fast for her to risk it.

Melissa again asked Tom where he was going and he told her he was taking them to the woods where he could cut their heads off and throw them into a creek. He drove down Bermuda Ave. and had stopped at a red light at the intersection of Bermuda and Broadway. While the truck was stopped, a police car pulled next to the passenger side of the truck. Amanda turned her head and looked out of the window. The policeman looked over at her and smiled. She nodded her head at him and turned her eyes toward Tom, trying to get the policeman's attention without alarming Tom. The light turned green and Tom accelerated slowly from the intersection. The policeman stayed with him for almost a mile. Tom told Amanda, "You try to get his attention again, and I will kill your fucking momma right now in the truck."

He pulled his buck knife from the sheath and placed it next to Melissa's abdomen. Amanda just looked out the window as the police turned away.

Tom drove six miles to a community in the southern part of County. It had been all swamp before it was developed. The community itself was in the boondocks. Tom turned off the main road just before reaching a long bridge. He drove for two or three more miles back into the woods and stopped at an opening a few feet from a creek. The moon hovered above, cascading streaks of dull light through the canopy of cypress trees. The murky creek water trickled southward with a blanket of rotting leaves and moss. The large cypress trees towered like skyscrapers above the shallow creek bed. Closer to the water line, large, ghost-like cypress knots extended from the ground. Just as Tom shut off the motor, there was a loud splash in the water. A six or seven foot long alligator whipped his tail across the surface.

He ordered both Amanda and Melissa out of the truck. He pointed to a grassy area next to the water and demanded, "You stand right there and don't fucking move!"

"What about alligators?" Melissa asked.

Tom opened a tool box that was mounted on the back bed of his truck and removed a large machete. "It's not going to matter in a few minutes," he said coldly as he removed a machete from its canvas cover and walked over to Amanda and Melissa.

Melissa began begging, "Oh no. Oh God, no, Tom, No!

Amanda joined in her mother's pleas, her voice breaking with fear and dread, "Please don't kill us, Tom. Please, I won't eat no more before we all eat."

"Get down on your damn knees and bend over!"

Melissa knelt down and began praying out loud, "Our Father, who art in Heaven!"

Amanda was hysterical, "Help us, somebody help us!" she cried desperately.

Tom took his foot and kicked Amanda off her knees and over on to her side, "Shut the fuck up!" Melissa instantly stopped praying out loud.

"Now go next to your Momma. Who wants to go first?"

Melissa was coughing and weeping uncontrollably. She put her arms around Amanda and said. "I'm sorry honey, I'm so sorry."
She suddenly pushed Amanda away and said to Tom. "Kill me first!"

Melissa bent over and extended her neck. Amanda screamed and put her arms around her mother, "NO!"

Tom pushed her away once again with his foot. Amanda put her head between her legs crying and pleading for Tom to stop.

Tom raised the machete above his head and held it there for a moment. "Are you ready to die?"

Melissa started praying again. Tom grunted, and then swung the machete downwards. Melissa braced herself for the blow to her neck. Tom swung past her and drove the blade into the ground. Amanda shrieked, not sure if she was alive or dead. Tom bent over and grabbed Melissa by her hair and stood her up in front of him. He picked the machete up from the ground and threw it into the creek. He pulled Melissa towards him forcing her to hug him and said, "Listen, you have to start being responsible, Missy. Hey, I am not going to kill you guys. Hell, I love both of you!"

Amanda was on the ground, stunned and in shock. Her mascara was smeared all over her face and she had dirt in her hair. Her eyes were red and engorged from crying for so long and so hard. Tom looked at her and asked. "What is that on your face? Are you wearing make-up?"

Melissa interrupted and said. "That's enough Tom!"

"All right. Come on, let's get in the truck and go home." Tom said as if nothing had just happened.

Amanda and Melissa got back into the truck, still crying and upset. Amanda looked out the window. It was dark and all she saw was her own reflection. She stared at herself for five minutes or so and made up her mind at that moment, "I am going to kill that bastard. I have had enough, that motherfucker is dead."

CHAPTER 43

Amanda discovers 38-caliber Pistol

Amanda didn't have many friends. Tom was extremely possessive and strict with her. His attitude around her friends usually scared them off, but Amanda met a young lady who she was able to befriend. Her name was Bridget Edwards. Bridget lived with her mother, Patricia Langley, in a mobile home on the banks of Shingle Creek.

They had similar personalities and many of their likes and dislikes were the same. Amanda and Robert from time to time would hang out at her house. Robert enjoyed going up and down the creek in Mrs. Langley's canoe.

Amanda had never confided to Bridget about her problems at home, but Bridget could tell when something wasn't right. If Amanda came to her house acting depressed, Bridget would press her to tell her what was wrong, but Amanda would just brush her off.

One night, Bridget was spending the night with Amanda and Tom started testing her to see how far she would permit him to go. He was poking her in the ribs and putting his arms around her in an overly-affectionate way. Amanda knew what he was doing and called him on it. She asked Tom if she could talk with him in private.

"What are doing? That's my friend!"

Tom looked at her, grinning, "What do you think? You think maybe I could get some from her?"

Amanda walked out of the room and took Bridget into her bedroom where they remained for the rest of the night.

After that incident Amanda didn't bring Bridget home with her any more.

On August 29, 1984, Amanda was visiting Bridget at her home.

"Do you know anything about guns?" Amanda asked Bridget.

"I know a little bit. My Dad is a hunter and he has lots of guns."

Bridget asked why she was asking questions about guns. "It just don't seem right for us not to have a gun in our house for protection," Amanda told her. "Does your Mom have a gun?"

"Sure! She keeps it right next to her bed," Bridget said.

"Really? Can I see it? I mean, can we look at it?" Bridget said, "Hmmm, I don't know. Mom doesn't allow me to handle her gun."

"She's not home right now, so let me look at it," Amanda said persuasively. She got up and started walking back to Bridget's mom's bedroom. "Okay, all right, you can look at it, but don't touch it," Bridget warned.

Bridget and Amanda went to her mother's room and Bridget opened a drawer in her mother's nightstand. Bridget picked up a Bible from the drawer and there was the gun.

"What kind of gun is that?" Amanda asked.

"I'm not sure, but I think it's a 38-caliber Chief's Special. My Dad bought it for my Mom for our protection." Bridget put the bible back in its place and closed the drawer.

That night when Amanda got home, she told Robert what she had learned.

"We can shoot Tom with that gun and it will all be over."

"I don't think a 38-caliber is big enough," Robert said. "I think we need a 357-magnum or a 44-magnum to make sure it does the job."

Amanda told him it was all they were going to be able to get. We just have to steal the gun when nobody's at home.

On September 1, 1984, Amanda was chatting with Bridget on the phone.

"We're going skating tonight," said Bridget. "Do you and Robert want to go with us?" Amanda asked who was going and

Bridget said that she and her little brother and Mom. "What time are you going?" Amanda asked.

"The session starts at eight o'clock, so we will get there at 7:45 on the dot." Bridget explained. Amanda told Bridget that she would like to go but would have to make sure it was okay with her parents.

When she hung up, she ran into Robert's room and said. "We go tonight, get ready. Bridget and her Mom are going to the skating rink at 7:45. I want you to go to the rink and wait and as soon as they arrive, call my beeper from the pay phone."

Robert and Amanda lived directly behind the skating rink, so Robert walked over just before 7:45 p.m. Amanda drove towards Bridget's house and parked in a wooded area next to a power station not more than a half mile from Bridget's trailer.

At 7:55 p.m., Amanda received a beep. She backed her car out of the power station and drove towards Bridget's house. It wasn't yet quite dark, but the sun was beginning to fade. She drove through an open gate and parked next to the trailer home. She tried to act like she was supposed to be there, just in case anyone was watching. Amanda pulled on the front door and discovered it was locked. She walked around the rear pulled on the rear door. Thankfully, it opened and Amanda walked in. She had entered the laundry room. She pulled the door closed behind her and walked into Patricia's bedroom. "This is spooky," she thought.

The phone rang and startled her. She opened the drawer and picked up the bible as the answering machine picked up and she heard the greeting, "Hi, this is Patricia; we can't come to phone right now, so please leave a message at the beep." She saw the gun right where Bridget had shown her. She picked it up, examined it for a minute, and then tucked it into her pants. She walked out of the room and was just about to leave the trailer, but suddenly remembered she had left the Bible on top of the night table. She returned and placed it back in the drawer.

She hid the gun under the seat in her car and drove to the skating rink. When Robert saw her he asked, "Did you get it?" Amanda just nodded her head and looked victorious.

CHAPTER 44
Caught in a Lie

"Listen to me. Can you just help me find a silencer?" Amanda asked. She was talking to a young black male, Harold Michaels, who was a prison inmate on work release assigned to Denny's Restaurant. "What's up with you, girl?" he asked in his neighborhood slang, "You going to eradicate that bastard?"

Amanda had explained to him weeks ago that her dad had been abusing her and her brother and she was not going to take it anymore.

"Girl you don't need no silencer, just shoot the bastard!" he exclaimed.

"Please, shh!" Amanda looked around anxiously to see if anyone was listening.

"Amanda, why don't you just call the police?' Harold asked.

Amanda explained that every time the police got involved things got worse. She explained about the Russian roulette game that Tom had played with her and Robert the first time.

"Damn, girl. That motherfucker is sick!"

Amanda looked up at Harold and asked, "Can you kill him for me?"

'Whoa, wait a damn minute, girl. I couldn't kill a fucking housefly." Harold said.

"I gotta get out of this place and killing a man sure won't help me a bit! Look, I know a dude up in the 'hood in O-town, he can set you up, but I need to go with ya."

They agreed to go the next day. If the inmate was missing for more than a couple of hours, he would be considered an escapee.

At 4:15 p.m. on September 4, 1984, Amanda and Robert left the house. Amanda told her mother they were going to visit friends in BVL. Amanda drove up to the rear of Denny's Restaurant. Harold was there waiting for her. Robert opened the door and Harold told him to get into the back seat. Harold sat down in the front next to Amanda.

"I needs me a beer or two, hey, stop at the 7-11," Harold ordered.

Amanda pulled into the 7-11 and Harold ran in and bought three cans of beer. As they drove off, Amanda asked, "Harold, do you know anyone who could do this for us?"

Harold told her he couldn't get involved in anything like that. They drove north on the Orange Blossom Trail until they reached Sand Lake Road. "Turn here," Harold told Amanda.

She turned left onto Sand Lake Road. "Okay, turn to the right at that 7-11 right there."

Amanda turned in and he told her to pull over. She stopped the car and Harold got out and walked up a group of young black males standing on the street corner.

"They look like drug dealers," Robert said.

Harold came back to the car and asked Amanda how much money she had.

"I got $100.00 with me right now," Amanda replied. Harold opened the car door and sat down in the front seat.

"Let's go! Keep going straight until we get to the white house with red shutters. Follow that homeboy."

A young black male was running on foot in front of them.

The black male ran up to a house with red shutters (where a drug dealer lived), and motioned for Harold to come with him. Harold and the black male walked up to the door and knocked. A voice behind the door said, "Who is it?"

Then the door opened and the black male said, "This is my homeboy. He is looking for a silencer for a 38-caliber Chief's Special."

"What the fuck!" The man behind the door said. "Get the fuck out of my house!"

"Come on man, hook me up! This bitch got the bread, man," the black male told him.

"Bring the bitch here."

Harold motioned for Amanda to come over. Robert and Amanda hesitantly walked up to the door. The drug dealer asked what Robert was there for. Harold told Robert to get back into the car. "What you want a silencer for, bitch?"

The drug dealer asked Amanda. Amanda explained that she just needed one. He told her he could get one, but would take a couple of days.

"It's going to cost you $500.00." he explained. "I ain't got $500.00!" Amanda replied.

"What you got?" he asked. Amanda told him she had only $100 and he told her to leave that with him and he would see if he could find something for her.

"No, I need it tonight!" She exclaimed. The drug dealer told her he couldn't help her.

"Let's go Amanda," Harold said.

They pulled out of the neighborhood and stopped at the 7-11.

"Now what?" Amanda asked.

"What time is it?" asked Harold.

Amanda replied it was nearly 6:00 p.m.

"You needs to get me back right away before I get in deep shit!"

Amanda dropped off Harold and headed home with Robert.

"What are we going to do?" Robert asked.

"I guess we just have to do it without a silencer," Amanda replied.

153

"Okay, Dad's not going to be home until late tonight, he has a meeting at the hotel." Amanda said.

When Amanda pulled her car into the parking lot, she saw Tom's truck in front of their apartment, "Oh shit! Oh my God!" Amanda said to Robert.

"He's here already. Okay, this is our story, we went to BVL and we visited our friends okay?"

"What about the gun?" Robert asked.

"We'll have to leave it in the car for now. We can't take it in there with Tom here," Amanda replied.

"We'll have to get it out later. Are you scared, Robert?"

"I've never been more scared in my entire life," he replied.

Amanda and Robert walked into the apartment and Melissa was sitting in the living room.

"Where's Dad?" Amanda asked as she threw her keys on to the coffee table.

"He's on the toilet," Melissa answered. Amanda walked to the bathroom and walked in without knocking.

"Hey, Dad," she said as she leaned forward and kissed him on the forehead.

Tom looked up at her and said, "Get the fuck out of here." He pushed her away and said with his hand.

"Me and your Mom, we been talking. We are taking our money and getting the fuck out of here. We ain't taking you and Robert. You are too fucking deceitful. You have pushed me too far. You have been walking all over me for too long! Now get out of here before I kill you!"

Amanda walked out of the bathroom. She stood next to the sliding glass door and then opened it quietly. "I have to get the gun right now," she thought. Robert saw her walk out and followed her.

"Get the gun now Robert!' Amanda whispered. Robert walked up to the car and attempted to open the door.

"It's locked." Robert said in a shaky, quiet voice.

"Oh shit, I never locked the car!" Amanda was mad at herself.

Amanda told Robert to stay there and she would in to get the keys. She opened the glass door and walked softly into the living room.

"Where are they?" she asked herself.

She frantically looked through the living room and the kitchen. Robert came back inside, fearing for Amanda.

Tom came out of the bathroom wearing his work pants and a white T-shirt. He had on white socks; one had a hole near the toe. He ordered both Robert and Amanda and to sit down on the sofa.

He looked at Amanda, "You think you're in for a free fucking ride don't you? You have a nice fucking car. You got nice fucking clothes and lots of spending money. What do you think this is? A luxury ride? Shit, you only work three hours a day." Tom sat down in his recliner and continued, "You ain't pulling your share of the whole nine yards!"

He looked at Robert, "Why ain't you at work?"

"They changed my schedule." Robert replied.

"I thought you were supposed to be there at 5:00 o'clock." Tom said. "I am so tired of them changing your schedule."

Tom sat there quietly as if he was thinking about what he was going to do. Robert and Amanda stood up and walked out of the living room.

The phone rang and Melissa answered it, "Hello. No, he is not supposed to be there tonight, his schedule was changed."

"Who is that?" Tom yelled.

"It's Robert's supervisor. She said he didn't show up for work tonight."

Tom took the phone from Melissa and said. "You people need to stop changing Robert's schedule. He can't make any money like this." Robert's supervisor told Tom that Robert was scheduled to work but he didn't show up. She told Tom he didn't call in either.

"I don't believe that." Tom said. "I am going to come down and look at the schedule right now, if that's all right with you."

Tom told Robert's boss. She said she could come on down and take a look, if he wished. Tom hung up the phone and there was a knock at the door. Tom had been trying to buy an A-frame house on Shingle Creek. The owner of the property was now here to discuss the sale. So Tom told Melissa to go to Burger King and look at the schedule.

Amanda and Melissa left in Melissa's car. When they arrived at Burger King, Amanda volunteered to go in and look at the schedule. When Amanda came back out she told her Mom that there was a pencil mark on the schedule that looked like Robert's day had been changed. Melissa told her to explain that to her father.

Tom was sitting at the kitchen table working on some numbers trying to decide if he could afford the house, when Amanda and Melissa got home.

"Well?" Tom asked.

Amanda said. "I went in and looked at the schedule, Dad. It did look like it was changed. I can see how Robert would have thought he was off today."

Tom picked up the phone and dialed the Burger King. Amanda asked, "Who are you calling?"

Tom told her he didn't believe her and that he was calling Burger King. The district manager picked up the phone and Tom asked her if the schedule was changed. The next thing Amanda heard was Tom apologizing, "I am very sorry, Candi. I am so sorry for this incident. Robert and Amanda both lied to me about the schedule. I am coming down there right now to apologize in person." Amanda heard that and thought, "perfect, we can bring the gun inside when he leaves."

Then Amanda heard, "Are you sure? I really don't mind coming down." Tom said.

156

Amanda's heart sank. He wasn't going after all.

"Robert and Amanda, come here right now!" Tom screamed.

Tom ordered them both to sit down on the sofa. Amanda, you just fucking lied to me again. That schedule ain't been changed at all. You fucking lie to me about such small shit. I can never trust you again. Robert, you been skipping work a lot. You just got fired, son."

Tom walked up to Robert and stood there towering above him. He was clicking his finger nails together. Robert's head was down. Tom turned away, and then twirled around swinging his open hand, striking Robert in the face. The impact knocked Robert from the sofa on to the floor. Robert screamed out for Tom to stop. "You damn liar!" Tom shouted. He reached down and picked up Robert by his hair and pushed him back on to the sofa.

"I can't trust you two. You are pieces-of-shit liars!" Tom yelled as he grabbed Amanda's hair.

He pulled her up to him yelling right in her face. He released her hair. Amanda was crying and pleaded with Tom to stop. He slapped Amanda in the face with his open palm, then again with the back of his hand.

"We are going to apologize to your boss, Robert. I am a man of honor and you are going to be, too." Tom yelled.

Amanda was thinking to herself, "Please go so I can get the gun out of my car."

Tom then announced, "Tomorrow we will go to Burger King. I can't believe it. Such a small thing, and you lie to me about it. It's not about not working, it's all about lying!'

Tom swung his hand, again striking Robert on top of his head. The impact caught Robert off-guard. He bit his lip as Tom's handmade impact with the top of his head.

Tom yelled for Melissa to come into the living room, "What time did these kids leave the house this afternoon?" Tom asked her. Melissa looked over at Amanda before she answered. "I thank it was somewhere around 4:30," she replied.

Tom looked back at Amanda and asked, "Now where were you for hours?" Amanda looked over at Robert and said, "We went to BVL, Dad."

Tom replied by spelling out the word Liar. He looked at Robert and repeated, "Where were you?" Robert's response was the same.

"I'll get to the bottom of this," Tom screamed.

He ordered them to follow him into the bedroom. "We're dead now," Amanda thought. They hadn't really gotten their stories together well enough to survive Tom's separate interrogations.

"Robert, you'd better tell me the truth this time, son.

" I did tell you the truth. Me and Amanda went to BVL and visited Bryan."

Tom interrupted and slapped Robert across the face. "I want the truth, damn it!"

"We went to BVL with that black guy from Amanda's work!" T

om picked the iron up from the ironing board and threw it at the wall. The iron crushed though the sheetrock and became lodged in the wall. Tom's face was red and he was losing total control. He pushed Robert out of the door and demanded for Amanda to come into the bedroom.

"Where were you tonight? I want the truth!" He ordered. Amanda gave him the same answer she had already given, "We went to BVL!"

Tom slapped her face. "You fucking whore, you were with a nigger. You fucking slut. What did you do? Fuck him? Damn, I want to fucking throw up!'

He grabbed Amanda's hair and slung her to the floor.

"Okay, Okay, Okay!" Amanda screamed. "We went to Orlando to buy a silencer!"

"You're still lying to me!" he said as he slapped Amanda again.

He told Amanda to leave the bedroom and called Robert back in. "Where were you tonight?" Tom asked Robert.

Robert's entire body was shaking. His voice was broken up but audible. "We went to Orlando to the circle. We went to a drug dealer's house!"

Tom was furious. "You went to a drug dealer's house? What happened?" Tom asked.

Robert told Tom that he didn't know. He explained that when he walked up to the door the black guy told him to go sit back in the car.

"What did Amanda do?" Tom asked.

Robert said, "She went inside. I couldn't see her."

Tom yelled, "Now I get it! Now it makes sense to me! Cocaine!"

Amanda was in the kitchen frantically searching the drawers for her keys and finally found a spare set. She put them in her pocket so the first chance she had, she could go get the gun.

Tom left Robert and went into the bathroom. Amanda ran outside and unlocked her car. She reached under the seat and pulled out the gun. She opened the cylinder to ensure there were bullets in the gun. When she opened the cylinder the bullets fell onto the floorboard. "Oh shit!" Amanda thought. She found five bullets and loaded them back into the gun.

She pushed the car door shut and went back in to the house. She picked up a sofa pillow and hid the gun underneath it. "When Robert comes out here he will find it." Amanda thought.

Tom yelled for Amanda to come into his bedroom. Amanda walked in and Tom started in on her, "You been fucking a nigger? How long you been doing this?"

Amanda yelled back "I ain't fucking no nigger, Tom. I told you we was looking for a silencer.

"Get the fuck out of my bedroom!" Tom yelled.

Amanda walked out and went directly to the sofa. She felt for the gun. "Oh my God, it's gone, Robert has it. He's going to do it right now. Oh my God! Oh my God!"

Her mind was whirling. She ran into the bathroom, turned on the water and flushed the toilet. She didn't want to hear the gun go off.

After a few minutes she turned off the water and walked back in the living room. She bent down and saw the gun under the sofa. She felt the hair on the back of her neck raise up. There was a shadow on the floor. Tom was standing behind her. "Does he see the gun?" she asked herself.

Amanda stood up straight and turned around. Tom was standing behind her. He was just standing there. He didn't say a word. Sometimes he would do that right before he hit the kids.

He looked at her and said, "Not worth it, was it?"

Amanda glanced up at him. His eyes were wild and his face was red and frightening. Amanda gasped and replied, "No it wasn't."

Robert was in his bedroom with the door locked. Tom attempted to open it and became more enraged when he discovered it was locked.

"Robert, unlock this damn door!" he shouted.

Robert opened the door and Tom told him to come into the living room.

Melissa complained she had a bad headache, so Tom gave her two pills that she thought were aspirin, but actually he gave her two valiums. He told her to go lay down in their bedroom. Then, he did something he had never done before. He took an old quilt form the linen closet and placed it across the top of the door and draped it downward in order to block noise.

Tom directed Amanda to sit on the loveseat and Robert to sit on the sofa.

"I have tried so hard to be a good father to both of you. I have given you everything. I just don't understand why you lie to me and cheat me the way you do. I've always tried to teach you both what's right and what's wrong, and you have chosen the wrong."

"Nothing seems to work," he said dramatically, as he sat down on the sofa. The heel of his foot was nudged against the gun. He felt his foot hit something and was about to look down when Amanda blurted out,

"We try to be good, dad, but sometimes when you tell one lie, you have to keep telling lies."

She was trying hard to take his attention away from what his foot had hit on the floor. Tom got angry when she said that. Robert had become a strong-willed individual, but was beginning to weaken under pressure. He had tears running down his face. He tried not to sniffle. The last thing he wanted was for Tom to detect his fear.

Tom stood up and walked into the kitchen, Amanda pointed to the gun, "Get it. Get it now!" she whispered.

Robert slid down towards the gun and sat on the end where it was placed. Amanda said it again, "Get it, Robert. You have to shoot him now." Robert was too nervous, and too scared to bend down and pick up the gun.

As he reached down under the sofa, Tom walked back into the living room. He had a pair of needle nose pliers in his hands. He took Amanda's hand and told her he was going to pull out her finger nails. He tried to grip her nails, but fortunately for her, she was a nail-biter and Tom couldn't get a grip on any of them. Amanda looked down at her hand and Tom kneed her in the jaw.

"Fuck!" he said.

He reached for Robert and twisted the pliers around a wad of Robert's hair. He jerked the pliers back and pulled out a clump of hair the size of a pencil. Robert screamed loudly in pain, and grabbed for his head. Tom grabbed another bunch of hair with the pliers and this time, a steady flow of blood flowed down the side of his head. Robert dropped on the floor and went into the fetus position to protect himself.

Tom threw the pliers on to the floor and pulled at Amanda's hair. He lifted her from the chair.

"This is a new trick!" Tom said to Amanda as she squirmed to break free.

Robert stood up and yelled for Tom to stop. He swung his fist at Tom, striking him on the back of the neck. Tom turned around and grabbed Robert by his ears. He lifted Robert from the floor until his left ear split and started bleeding.

Tom heard a car door close and he jumped up and looked out the window. He locked the front door and returned.

Robert said, "You're not a man to pick on two kids!"

Tom reacted by kicking Robert under his chin, as if he were kicking a football. Robert fell back against the wall and Tom kicked him in the chest, temporarily stopping his breathing. Robert gasped for air and fell onto the floor.

Tom started pacing back and forth in the house. He was mumbling things that didn't make any sense.

Robert was able to stand up and catch a breath.

"Liars, liars, liars!" Tom kept repeating.

He grabbed Robert's shirt. "You like this shirt? You like this shirt, boy?" Robert replied, "Yes, sir!"

Tom pulled it apart breaking the buttons loose. He then pulled the sleeves in opposite directions until it ripped in half. Tom pulled the shirt up and proceeded to choke Robert with it.

"Stop it! Stop it!" Amanda screamed.

She threw a lamp at him and struck Tom on the back. Robert's face was blue. Tom dropped Robert and turned towards Amanda.

"Okay, bitch. You like your fucking Hang Ten shirt and OP shorts?" Tom said as he ripped Amanda's shirt off of her.

He pulled at her shorts and ripped them off, as well. "Now what are you going to do?" Tom asked. Amanda was standing there in her bra and panties. He ripped her bra off, tearing the snaps in the back. He reached out and started twisting and pinching Amanda's breast. "You like this!" he yelled, "Is this the kind of treatment you get when you're with a nigger? You like it, damn it?."

"No sir! Amanda screamed as loud as she could. Tom slapped her and told to shut up.

"I need some water!" Tom said. He walked towards the kitchen again.

Upon his return he said, "I am going to get this straight if I have to beat both of you for forty straight hours!"

He sat down on in his recliner and started watching TV and Melissa walked into the living room. Amanda asked her mom (who was barely awake and under the influence of the valiums) if she could go get some clothes on. Melissa said she could and Amanda ran to her room. Tom looked up and asked where she was going. Melissa told him that she was going to put some clothes on.

"She ain't putting none of my clothes on!" he shouted.

Amanda heard Tom shout out that she wasn't allowed to put on his clothes, so she put on a pair of shorts and T-shirt that belonged to Melissa.

Amanda walked out of the house to her car. She opened the driver's side door and reached under the seat for the gun. Her heart stopped when she couldn't find it.

"Oh shit, it's in the house already." She had forgotten she had already taken it into the house. She went back inside and sat on the sofa with her feet on the coffee table. Robert was sleeping, sitting up, on the love seat.

Tom walked in and said, "This ain't the end. It ain't over yet, I'm going to get the bottom of this shit tonight!"

Tom sat down next to Amanda and told her to take her feet off the coffee table. He picked up the remote and changed the channel on the TV. Tom looked at the TV and didn't take his eyes off it for twenty or thirty minutes.

Then out of nowhere, he says to Amanda, "So you like cocaine, huh?" Amanda responded, "Yeah."

Tom stood up and started to laugh and walked into the kitchen. Amanda heard him open a cabinet then close it.

"So you like to get high?" Tom shouted.

He walked back into the living room with a box of baking soda and a teaspoon. He dipped the spoon into the baking soda and put the spoon up to Amanda's nose.

"Snort this shit!" He said.

Amanda looked at him and told him she didn't want to snort the baking soda. Tom flipped the spoon and tossed the baking soda in Amanda's face. Most of it went into her eyes.

"You think you're so fucking smart, don't you?" Tom asked Amanda. "Snorting cocaine and fucking niggers."

Tom put the spoon back into the box and filled it with a heap of baking soda. His face expression suddenly changed along with his voice. It was like a different person was talking. He dropped the box on the floor and grabbed Amanda's face and held the spoonful of baking soda up to her nose.

"Snort this right now, damn it! Right fucking now!"

He shoved the spoon into her nostril and Amanda sniffed at the soda. "Snort it, damn it!" Tom screamed.

Amanda snorted real hard and the entire spoonful of soda went into her nostril. She started gagging and coughing.

"I can't do this!" Amanda cried.

Tom picked up the box and told Amanda that was only one nostril. "Now, you have to do the other side, too! You want to use cocaine, huh?" He shoved another spoonful of baking soda into her other nostril. Amanda started choking and gagging. Tom turned her and hit her on the back.

"Did that nigger sell you that cocaine?" Tom asked. Amanda responded, "Yes sir!"

Tom drew his hand back and slapped Amanda in the face calling her a slut, a cokehead and a nigger fucker. The impact caused Amanda to lose her balance and fall backwards onto the floor. She blew her nose out onto the carpet and saw the gun under the sofa. She was thinking, "If I don't do it now, he may kill me tonight."

She looked up at Robert and he was looking down at her. He shook his head back and forth telling her no. Amanda decided she was going to go for it. As soon as she made up her mind, Tom grabbed her from behind.

"You want to snort crazy shit?"

He had a can of black pepper in his hand and poured at least half the can into his hand. He pulled Amanda's face to his hand and held the pepper up to her nose forcing her to inhale. Pepper went into Amanda's eyes, up her nose and in her mouth. She turned away and threw up on the floor. She ran to the bathroom and tried to wash the pepper out of her eyes.

Tom followed her into the bathroom and continued screaming and yelling at her.

"You think snorting cocaine is all right, don't you?"

Amanda tried to talk but she had black pepper and baking soda in her throat. Tom pulled at her hair, causing her to once again lose her balance. Amanda fell up against the sink and got a gash above her right eye. She was physically exhausted. She dropped on to the floor and curled up in the fetal position. Tom opened the medicine cabinet and removed a bottle of Orajel and a bottle of Anbesol. Both were medicines normally used for toothaches. He left the bathroom with both bottles.

Amanda stayed on the floor until he left the room. She stood up and turned on the shower. She locked the door, and then removed her mother's clothes.

Amanda stepped into the shower and put her face under the hot water. The heat felt good as she blew her nose. She shampooed her hair and washed herself. She made the water hotter and just stood there enjoying the effects of the hot water. She started crying and wished she had never been born. "I just can't take this anymore," she cried.

Amanda stepped out and grabbed a towel. She placed the warm towel to her face and inhaled, and then she dried herself off. She put her dirty panties in the clothes hamper, and put her mother's shorts and T-shirt back on.

When she got back into the living room, Tom was watching TV again and Robert was sleeping.

Tom looked at her and said, "We ain't through yet, girl! Not by a long shot!"

Amanda started crying and put her head down. She screamed, "That's enough!" begged Amanda.

Tom looked at her and said, "I decide when it's enough, and I say it ain't enough yet, cause you ain't learned your lesson!'

He had a Visine bottle in his hand. He sat down and commenced to pour Orajel into the bottle. He was spilling most of it on to the coffee table. He put down the Orajel and picked up a bottle of Anbesol. After emptying both bottles into the Visine bottle, he ordered Amanda to snort it. He said, "You want to get numb don't you? This will get you numb. This will make you high!" he muttered.

He pulled Amanda to him and sprayed the mixture up into her nose. Amanda didn't sniff when he sprayed the bottle so Tom slapped her.

"Sniff, damn it!" he yelled. He sprayed into Amanda's other nostril and forced her again to sniff.

Amanda's throat and tongue were numb. She tasted the Orajel and Anbesol. The taste was nasty when mixed with the Visine, but not as bad as the black pepper.

Tom threw the bottle on the floor and said, "That's real good for you, ain't it?" Then, as if someone suddenly turned him off, he sat down next to Robert and started watching TV again.

It was 11:30 p.m. and Melissa woke up. She walked into the living room and Tom told her to go back to bed. He escorted her back to bed. Tom walked back into the kitchen and got a glass of water and two more valium. Amanda could hear him telling Melissa, "Everything is okay, honey. You just go back to sleep."

Amanda was sitting just above the gun, rocking her body back and forth. She whispered to Robert, "Wake up Robert; we have to do it now." Robert just shook his head. Amanda asked, "Why not?" Robert said, "I can't, not right now!"

A few minutes later Tom came back into the room. He walked up to Robert and hit him on top of his head. Robert looked up at him. Tom asked, "Are you sleepy, Robert?"

The only response Robert gave was a head nod, indicating he was sleepy.

"None of this shit bothers you, does it?" Tom asked Robert. Robert just nodded his head. "Let me tell you this, Robert Jenkins, "If you go to sleep, I am going to kill you." Robert sat there and a tear ran down his cheek. He wiped it off with his hand.

"Oh now you're going to be a crybaby! Let me tell you, it's easy to kill someone in their sleep. You see, all you got to do is get a big plastic garbage bag and put it over their head while they're sleeping. When the police do their autopsy it just shows that the person had a heart attack."

Robert started crying. He felt bad about crying because he was showing weakness in front of Tom, but he just couldn't control it.

"Why don't you go on to bed, son?" Tom asked. He told Robert he wouldn't even feel it. "I'll wait until you are in a deep sleep. It won't even hurt," Tom said in a devilish voice.

Robert didn't move. He didn't dare go to bed. He felt strongly that Tom would kill both him and Amanda tonight unless they killed him first.

Suddenly, there were red and blue flashing lights in the front window. A police car had stopped in the road behind a car. They could hear the policeman talking to the driver of the car. Tom jumped up and pulled the curtains tight together. He stood next to the window until the lights stopped flashing and the police car left.

Robert was sitting on the loveseat fighting sleep. His eyes were closing and re-opening and his head was bobbing to the left and right.

Tom walked up to him and tapped him on the shoulder. "I'm not going to kill ya. You go on ahead and go to bed, Robert," he whispered.

Robert stood up and walked to his bedroom. He lay on his back, but kept his eyes open as long as he could. Just before he dozed off, he said a prayer.

"Dear God, I know it was wrong for me to kill that little squirrel for no reason and I still feel bad today for doing it. I don't know if there is a heaven, but I guess I won't be allowed there if I kill a person and I'm scared. I am scared I won't be able to pull that trigger and Tom will kill me and Amanda and claim we tried to kill him. Please give me the strength tomorrow to point that gun at him and kill him. Amen"

After his prayer, Robert went to sleep. Tom held up his hand, extending his middle finger towards Amanda. "You ain't nothing but a little bitch," he said.

Amanda started crying again. Tom sat down next to her and asked, "Why are you still crying?" Amanda didn't look up him so Tom moved over to the love seat and picked a magazine and began thumbing through it. He put it down and started watching the news. Other than the TV, the room was quiet for thirty minutes.

Tom turned away from the TV and looked towards Amanda and said, "I ain't mad at you no more."

Amanda looked up at him and asked,

"What did you say?" Tom smiled at her and said, "I ain't mad at you no more, honey."

"Do you forgive me? Come on, do you?" he asked, jokingly. Amanda responded with, "Okay, I forgive you."

Tom held out his arms and asked for a hug. Amanda stood up and walked over to Tom. She bent down and hugged him putting her arms around his back.

Tom said, "You know I love you, don't you Amanda? I just don't want you doing something stupid like using cocaine."

Tom started caressing Amanda's neck, then massaging her shoulders. He placed his lips against her the back of her neck and kissed her, moving very slowly. He stroked his lips up and down her neck onto her shoulders. Amanda sat there and didn't move. Tom lifted her T-shirt over her head and dropped it on the coffee table. He started massaging her shoulders again and then unhooked her bra. He slowly took her bra off. Her breasts were exposed. Tom caressed his hands over her breast and squeezed both of them. "You know, Amanda I love you. You are almost eighteen years old now. We can have a baby, you and me," Tom whispered into Amanda's ear. "We can leave your Mom and move away together. You know me and your Mom ain't been having sex lately and you and me, hell, we fit together like two bugs in a rug," Tom said, trying to be funny.

He pulled down her shorts and exposed Amanda's pubic hair. "Oh my God, you are so beautiful," he said, as he ran his fingers through her pubic hair. Tom started grunting and moaning and removed his work pants and boxer underwear. Amanda reached out and grabbed his penis in her hand. Tom immediately got an erection.

Tom jumped up from the loveseat and went into his bedroom. He returned with a tube of KY jelly and filled his hand with the lubricant. "Lay down, baby," he ordered.

Amanda laid back and spread her legs as Tom smeared the KY Jelly in and around the outside of her vagina. "I love you baby," he whispered to Amanda as he mounted and entered her. Tom started out slowly, and then increased the intensity of his thrust. He was kissing Amanda as he pumped. Sweat dripped from Tom's forehead onto Amanda's chest.

Amanda was thinking she had to save his sperm this time to prove he had sex with her.

As Tom was reaching his climax, he asked Amanda if she, too, was coming. "Yeah!" Amanda lied. Amanda began thrusting her hips as if she was climaxing. Tom finished and laid there with his arm around Amanda. Both of them fell asleep.

CHAPTER 45

Rehearsal How to Kill Dad

Amanda opened her eyes and looked around. Tom was sleeping next her. "God, he stinks!" Amanda thought to herself. She was completely naked in between Tom and the back of the sofa. Amanda shook Tom and told him to wake up.

Tom jumped up and began cursing right away. "Damn it, what time is it? The clock didn't go off, or what?" Tom ran down the hallway to the bathroom. He didn't bother to put on any clothes.

He started talking to himself saying, "I was going to quit anyway, maybe I'll just stay home and say to hell with it. No, that's not very honorable."

He picked up the phone and called his boss. "I'm so sorry, but we must have had a power outage last night. My clock is blinking and my alarm didn't go off this morning. I'm headed in right now," he said.

Tom was showered and out the door in fifteen minutes. Amanda woke up her mother and told her the alarm didn't go off. Melissa was still sleeping in her work clothes from the previous day. Amanda woke up Robert and told him that Tom was gone. "What are we going to do?" Robert asked Amanda. She told him they needed to wait until their mother left for work then they could make start planning.

Melissa was leaving at 11:00 a.m. and suddenly stopped in her tracks. She looked back and saw Amanda standing in the living room next to the sofa.

"What happened last night?" she asked.

Amanda told her, "You don't want to know."

She was working the first shift at Red Lobster. When she arrived, she told her boss and friend, "I just don't know, something isn't right today. I can feel it in my bones"

Meanwhile, Amanda and Robert removed the gun from under the sofa.

"Here, Robert. Hold it. Get the feel of it, so you it won't feel awkward this afternoon. Listen, we have to make a plan. It has to look like self-defense or we will go to jail forever. Hell, we might even get the death penalty," Amanda said.

Robert opened the cylinder, removed the bullets and placed them in his pants pocket.

"I don't care if I get the death penalty, Amanda. I am willing to take that chance," he said.

"You know, we have no other choice. If we run away from him, he will find us. If we call the police he will pay them off, like last time. He will probably take us to that swamp and cut our heads off," Robert pondered, shuddering at the thought.

He pointed the gun at his image in the mirror and pulled the trigger.

"I'm ready," he said. "So, what's the plan?"

Amanda sat down with him and said, "We have to do this right. I think we should use the iron and, okay, you will use the, iron and burn my face with it. You will have to hold it to my face," she explained.

"We need to throw the iron into the wall afterwards; and, you know, and make a hole," Robert said.

Amanda emphasized to Robert that what they were about to do was going to be very dangerous. "If you miss, he will kill us both tonight, here in this apartment and no one will know our story. So you have to shoot him in the head. Shoot him with all six bullets, okay?" Amanda said.

"Okay, the iron ..." started Robert. He was getting confused. Amanda interrupted, "I will write it down for you, okay?" She removed a piece of white stationery from the kitchen drawer and wrote down the following list:

1. Burn my face with the iron
2. Throw iron into the wall
3. Hit Robert in the face with a belt, making welts
4. Break the pottery on the coffee table
5. Fall back into the wall and make a large hole with my body
6. Put the clump of Robert's hair from last night on to the floor

   in front of the loveseat with the pliers

They planned the exact location Tom needed to be in order for Robert to shoot him. Amanda walked into the kitchen and stood next to the refrigerator. She surveyed the view from there and told Robert this is where he should hide the gun, "Listen Robert, we have to do this as soon as he comes home. If he finds this gun, we are in a world of shit," Amanda said.

She drew a picture of the living room and then added the furniture.

Robert told her, "I think I should come out of the bathroom and you just get up, get out of the way when I come out."

"NO!" Amanda was adamant. he might see you with the gun coming down the hallway! I will sit here," she said, pointing to the center of the sofa. "I will have him sit next to me and help me with my unemployment papers. He will sit right here and face this direction," She pointed towards the front door.

"As soon as you notice him looking down, you walk into the kitchen and open the refrigerator. You take the gun out of the towel and walk towards us. Shoot him in the head. If you don't, it may not kill him," Amanda instructed.

"Okay, everything is set. Let's practice, okay?"

Amanda and Robert practiced just how they were going to destroy once and for all the source of their abuse and torture for so many years. They were determined it would all end today. They were not going to endure another night of agony at the hands of Charles Thomas Jenkins.

Robert went into the bathroom and wrapped the gun in a white hand towel and hid it between the refrigerator and the cabinet.

Amanda asked Robert if he wanted to go get something to eat. He was so nervous that he said he didn't think he could eat anything. We need to eat and then get our stories together. We have to give exactly the same story or we are dead," Amanda explained. Amanda drove them to Burger King and they sat inside and each had a Whopper Meal.

"This might be our last meal together, Amanda," Robert said. "If we go to jail we may not see each other again." A big tear ran down Robert's cheek.

"I just want you to know that I love you, sis. You have always been the best sister I could ever ask for." They stood up and hugged each other.

"I love you too, Robert. I always have, little brother," she said. "Now let's go and get ready."

They returned to the apartment at 3:30 p.m. and Amanda spread her unemployment papers out on the coffee table. They were both extremely nervous anticipating what was about to happen.

"Robert, he has beaten us for nine years. This is the right thing, I promise you," Amanda said confidently.

Robert looked at her and said, "I know, but I'm scared, Amanda!" He began to cry. Amanda started crying with him.

Robert asked, 'What about mom, what's going to happen to her?" "Don't worry about Mom. She can live again after today," Amanda responded.

The phone rang. Amanda rushed to pick it up. "Hello," she said as she placed the phone to her head. It was Tom,

"Hey, Amanda. Listen, I called the prison and talked to the warden. We have to go out there tomorrow so you can make a statement."

Amanda asked, "Why do I have to do that?"

Tom explained she needed to write a statement stating the inmate had provided her with cocaine. "The warden said they would lock him down and return him to regular prison, if that's the case. I want that bastard put away for a long fucking time."

Amanda listened and said, "Okay Dad. I'll sign a statement."

Tom said he was leaving work right then and would be home around 5:00 p.m.

"Why don't you heat up that spaghetti in the refrigerator and put some rolls in the oven and we can eat it when I get home." Tom said.

"Sure, Dad, but I need your help with these unemployment papers 'cause I can't figure them out, okay?" Amanda told him.

Tom hung up. He was in a good mood and it sounded like everything was back to normal.

Robert yelled, "We gotta to burn your face and put the holes in the wall!"

Amanda told him they couldn't do that until afterwards. "If dad comes in and sees that, he will know something is wrong."

"That's true." Robert agreed.

They sat in the kitchen and waited. Both were staring at the wall clock. It was so quiet in the house; they could hear the click of each movement of the secondhand.

"I can feel my heart beating," Robert said. Amanda replied that she, too, could feel her heart pounding.

At five o'clock, Amanda reached out and shook Robert's hand. Robert stood up and walked into the back of the house.

Tom was never late. If he said five he would arrive at five on the dot. Robert was standing in the bathroom listening. He put his hands in his pocket and his heart skipped a beat. "The bullets, the fucking bullets, they're still in my pocket, oh shit!" he thought. He ran down the hallway into the kitchen. He heard Tom's truck pull up out front. A neighbor was out front and Tom started talking with him.

Robert unwrapped the gun and opened the cylinder. His hands were shaking so badly, he couldn't line up the bullets. He dropped two on the floor. He could hear Tom walking towards the front door. Robert bent over and picked up one of the bullets and kicked the other one under the refrigerator. He managed to get four into the chamber and then Tom opened the front door. Robert closed the cylinder and re-wrapped the gun up in the towel.

Amanda greeted Tom as he entered the apartment.

"Hey, Dad." Robert was having difficulty swallowing. His mouth was like cotton. The artery on his neck was thumping.

"Hey, here are all the papers I told you about," Amanda said, pointing to the papers on the coffee table.

"Can you help me?"

Tom walked away from her and headed to his bedroom. He opened the door then went into his master bathroom. He stood at the toilet and urinated. He left the door open and Amanda stood in the doorway, talking to him.

"I just didn't realize there was so much paperwork needed to file unemployment," Amanda said.

Tom followed her back to the living room and Amanda sat down in the spot she had prepared and motioned for Tom to sit next to her. Tom told her to wait a minute.

"I need to get me a beer," he said. He walked towards Robert in the kitchen and Robert said, "I'll get it for you." Robert removed a beer from the refrigerator and handed it to Tom.

Tom walked back and sat next to Amanda. He bent over and started reading a form out loud. Sweat was running down

Robert's pant legs as he reached behind the refrigerator and unwrapped the 38-caliber Chief's Special. He looked at the gun for a second, swallowed hard, and then turned towards Tom and Amanda. His hands were shaking to the point he could hardly aim the weapon. He remembered he needed to breathe and squeeze.

Robert looked at his father's back and started crying. He lifted the gun up to his line of sight, "Breathe and squeeze," he told himself.

Amanda looked back and saw what he was doing and screamed out, "No, Robert!"

Tom looked back and saw Robert standing behind him with the gun and yelled out, "No!"

Then, with a thunderous explosion, the gun went off. The recoil and noise startled Robert and he fell back. The bullet slammed into Tom's back thrusting him forward as if he had just been kicked by a horse. As Tom tried to recover, he stood up and picked up a black antique iron from the floor and threw it at Robert. Tom missed and it hit the kitchen wall. Robert leveled the gun at him again.

"Oh my God, please don't, son!" Tom screamed out. He turned to run.

Robert's eyes were watering, but he still squeezed the trigger and, with another thunderous explosion, sent a second bullet into his father's left rear shoulder. The force of the second bullet thrust Tom into the wall. He stumbled over a lamp and fell to the floor. Amanda continued screaming for Robert to stop. She was hysterical, yelling and shrieking. Tom staggered towards the door trying to get away from his son. Robert leveled the gun and fired a third time. The bullet shattered the door facing. Tom tripped and fell once again as he struggled to get through the front door.

Tom stumbled out of the doorway, pleading for someone to hear him.

"Help me! Amanda! Help me!" he begged.

He was alone. No one was there to even hear his pleas. He clutched his chest, gasping for each breath. He fell again, this time on to a concrete planter just outside the front door of their apartment. He was unable to use his hands to cushion his fall. His right ear slammed into the corner of the planter base. The pain was as intense as the fiery hot bullets slamming into his back and chest. Somehow he managed to stand up once again. Blood oozed from his back and ran at a steady pace down his shirt. His ear was torn and blood trickled onto his shoulder.

"Oh my God, Oh my God!" Tom repeated.

He walked, hunched over, through the parking lot and on to the grass lawn. He turned his head back towards his apartment, looking for Robert. He yelled out Amanda's name, but no sound came out of his mouth. He turned and walked towards the street and fell face first onto the grass.

Robert ran as fast as he could to the Red Lobster Restaurant where his Mother was working. He burst through the entranceway and yelled, Mom! Mom!" Melissa was waiting on a customer, she was holding a plate in her hand and dropped it to the floor when she heard Robert's cry.

"Mom I did it. I shot him, I shot him three times, but I don't think he's dead. He's going to kill me, I know it!" Robert screamed. Melissa said, "You did what? Wait a minute," Melissa said. "I'll get you a ride to Patricia's house. You stay there until I call you, okay?"

Robert was breathing hard to the point of hyperventilating. Melissa hugged him and sent him on his way. Melissa asked a co-worker to drive him to Patricia Langley's house on Crawford Drive, the very same house that he and Amanda had stolen the gun from.

When Robert arrived, Bridget Edwards, Patricia's daughter and Amanda's friend, was home. He told her he had just shot his father. "Can you take me down the river in your canoe to somewhere I can hide?" Robert asked. "If he finds me, he will kill me!"

Bridget took Robert into her backyard. They pushed the canoe in the creek. The water was dark and dismal. It was a popular hangout for alligators. Bridget paddled south for five or ten minutes until they came to a small dock in front of a mobile home. Robert jumped up and pointed to a clump of bushes.

"I will stay right there. Can you bring me a blanket?" he asked. Bridget replied she would try, but might not be able to come back out. Robert walked over to the bushes and Bridget pushed the canoe back out into the creek.

"Good luck!" She called out to him.

"I can't stay here," Robert thought to himself, as he started walking deeper into the woods. The sound of frogs croaking along the bank frightened him. The next step he took, he sank into mud, and when he lifted his foot up, he lost his shoe. It was dark at that point and he could barely see where his shoe had lodged into the mud. When he retrieved the shoe, it was filled with wet, runny mud and it stunk. "Phew!" he said out loud. He backed up and banged the shoe against a cypress stump and then put it back on.

He turned around and headed in what he thought was the same direction he had just come. He could hear people talking. "Oh shit, that's Dad!" he thought as he knelt down to conceal himself. He listened for a minute and was able to discern that the voices he heard did not include his father's. He continued walking and found a clearing. It was a railroad track. He decided to walk down the track but he was now totally disoriented. When he came out to the road it was half a block from his house. He saw headlights coming his way. The car sounded like a Z-28 so he ran for cover. Robert hid behind a pine tree until the car passed.

He decided he needed to go to a friend's house, but wasn't sure exactly how to find it. He followed the railroad track and walked for about two miles until he recognized the area. He ran through several yards, jumping over fences, until he arrived at his friend's house. He knocked on the door and his friend Sidney answered, "Robert, what the…" Robert quickly interrupted him,

"I shot my ole man and he's after me. Do you know anywhere I can hide?"

His friend Sidney took him to a special place he knew in the woods where Robert remained until the next day. Robert climbed up a huge oak tree and stayed sitting on a large limb wide-awake until the next morning. When the sun came up, Robert walked into a convenience store and bought a honey bun. He used a pay phone to call his house, but there was no answer. His arms were itching and covered in mosquito bites. He decided it was too dangerous to hang around the store, so he went back into the woods.

Somewhere around 3:00 o'clock p.m., Robert went back to the store and called his house again, but there was still no answer. He called Bridget's house and Bridget picked up the phone.

"Hello," she said as she placed the phone to her ear.

Robert was quiet at first and Bridget again said, "Hello, who is this?"

Robert replied, "It's me."

"Robert, where are you? Are you okay? Where are you?" said Bridget.

Robert told her he didn't want to say. Bridget's mother Patricia Langley asked Bridget if that was Robert. Bridget nodded. Patricia took the phone from Bridget.

"Robert, this is Mrs. Langley, are you okay?"

Robert responded, "Yes Ma'am, "but ..." Robert stopped talking, his throat swelling as he began to cry.

"Son, where are you? Let me come get you," Patricia said.

Robert asked, "Where's my dad?"

"Son, your father is dead. He is never going to hurt you again." Patricia explained.

Robert was overwhelmed with emotion and began weeping hysterically on the phone. "I'm at the store on Thacker Avenue at the railroad track," he said. Patricia told him she had some very good friends who worked at the police department and she would call them to help.

Patricia picked him up and took him home with her. She called the Police Department and two officers were dispatched. Robert was taken into custody and transported to me.

CHAPTER 46
911 Call

    After the shooting, Amanda left the apartment and knocked on a neighbor's door. He let her in and she called the police department.

    The following is a transcript of the telephone conversation between Amanda and the 911 dispatcher.

    P signifies the police dispatcher and G signifies Amanda.

P. Police Department

G. Is this the police?

P. Police Department

G. Oh, please get over to Charra Condominiums E-1, there's been a death, and somebody's been shot in our apartment. Please hurry!

P. Somebody's been shot?

G. Yes

P. Okay hold on, Charra Condominiums E-1. Um did this just happen?

G. Yes, will you hurry?

P. Ma'am, just settle down, okay, ma'am? Chara Condos Apt E-1?

G. Yeah!

P. What is your address?

G. Apartment A-1. Please contact the damn police!

P. Ma'am, the ambulance is on the way. What is your address? Is it 1044

G. What?

P. What is your phone number, ma'am?

G. Charra Condominiums

P. Okay, ma'am. We have the police on the way

G. Good. Okay.

P. Is the subject still there with the gun, ma'am?

G. Please, just get me an ambulance and everything quick!

P. Okay, listen.

G. I'm not there and I ain't going back there.

P. Did you come home and discover this? Is the subject still there with the gun?

G. I don't know!

P. Do you know the person…

G. I ran to my friend's and I'm just over here.

P. Ma'am, ma'am

G. Yes

P. Do you know the person who is dead?

G. I don't know if anybody is dead!

P. Okay

G. He was shot two or three times and I ran and I went back in the house

P. Okay, did he shoot himself?

G. No! He didn't shoot himself, somebody shot him

P. Okay, Ma'am

G. When the police get here I'll …

P. Ma'am, is the subject still on the scene?

G. What?

P. Is he still there?

G. I don't know, I left

Static sound on the line …

P. Ma'am, ma'am. What is your name?

G. Yes, it's Amanda Jenkins

P. What is your phone number?

G. I'm not there!

P. Okay, what's the number where you are?

G. Listen, this guy has been shot four or five times and this guy has a knife and he is probably going to kill this other guy.

P. Hello, ma'am. Hello, we have an officer on the scene, ma'am. Hello?

    After the call to the 911 dispatcher, Amanda left her neighbor's apartment and ran on foot to the Restaurant where her mother worked and told her mother what had happened. She told her she was sure Tom was already at the hospital. Melissa's boss, Kelly St. Francis, drove the two of them to the hospital where we all met.

CHAPTER 47

The Grand Jury Investigation

Over the next month or so, in addition to the public defender, my investigative partner and I became Amanda and Robert's most diligent allies. We were determined to learn the truth about these kids' pasts and I was pretty sure these kids would be vindicated.

I was extremely concerned about Melissa Jenkins. Our investigation in Tennessee had opened a can of worms about her, as well. It was evident she had participated in the rape of Anne Jones with Tom Jenkins and that she had been involved for nearly a decade in incestuous acts of sexual battery and child abuse of her own children. We knew Tennessee had a warrant for her and Tom, but they were not interested in enforcing it as long as she was in Florida.

I decided to question Amanda without her mother present. I told her, "Listen Amanda, I've been straight with you since this whole thing started. I need to know about any sexual contact that you or your brother Robert may have had with your mom since you've been in Florida."

Amanda said, "Whatever my Mom did, it was because she was afraid Tom would kill her and us." She said her mother was as much of a victim as they were. Amanda made it clear to me the issue of her mother was off-limits.

I interviewed Robert and his statement regarding his mother was a carbon copy of Amanda's statement. Detective John Singleton and I met with Lieutenant Bartholomew and discussed the issue of Melissa. We went through all the investigative reports and statements and we just couldn't find any evidence of incest involving Melissa since they arrived in Florida.

We bounced back and forth on that issue. I just felt like she had a responsibility to protect her children against her husband. She appeared to very passive, but as a mom you would think she would have risked her own life to save her kids from constant abuse.

"You guys are forgetting one thing here," an uninvolved detective said to us. "These two kids murdered somebody. They took a life. They need to be punished. Do we want to send a message to kids that it's okay to shoot your parents if they get a little rough? It's not likely that anyone is going to know exactly what these kids went through that led to this."

I looked at him and said, "Get the hell out of here! This has nothing to do with you."

The newspapers covered Tom's funeral and made a point out of the fact the kids didn't attend. Who in the world would expect the kids to attend that funeral? I didn't go, either. According to the news coverage, basically the only people who did attend were Melissa and a couple of Tom's relatives.

The kids were assigned a guardian ad Litem by the state who watched over their every move. She also spent a lot of time with Melissa.

The county had become a magnet for local and national news agencies. This murder was top headlines in the local news papers. Every time the kids had to appear in court the news cameras and reporters swarmed on the courthouse.

Preparing this case required hundreds of man hours from a variety of investigative sources. The public defender's office, the medical examiner, crime scene technicians, and our team of investigators were working around the clock.

Shortly after the shooting, Melissa and the kids moved out of the apartment and into a 3-bedroom home..

Our investigation was intense. I don't think we left any stones unturned. The information we brought back from Tennessee clearly indicated why the children didn't seek assistance from the police or HRS for that matter. We were all shocked at the abuse Amanda and Robert had endured.

It looked to me like Tom got just what he deserved. I think I would have treated him differently in the ambulance, if I had had a clue.

Less than a month after the shooting, Amanda was arrested in Orlando at Mall. She had attempted to use one of Tom's credit cards. I guess she was trying to get as much out of him as she could before it was too late.

We had been holding meetings almost daily with the state attorney to plan how the state should proceed with this case. Everyone knew the life story of both kids by now. The problem we were facing was the Grand Jury. The state has to present all homicides to the Grand Jury. They would make their decision based only on the information presented by the state attorney. There are no defense attorneys at this juncture.

I was stuck with presenting my case for the prosecution and based on the information I had so far, I was certain there would be a first degree murder indictment. I could only hope that that cooler heads would prevail.

I received my subpoena and was as prepared as anyone could be. I was very concerned about the incriminating note Amanda had written and, of course, the gun. It looked like it was pre-meditated murder. Had they stolen the gun to use in self-defense and used it during one of Tom's torturous episodes, there wouldn't even be a question.

I testified before the Grand Jury for six hours. The state attorney, Larry Vaughn hit everything. This guy was like a machine. He was ruthless. He was the type of prosecutor the police always wanted on their case. He had a track record of wins and he was on track with this one. However, he had children, too, and I could tell the circumstances in this case were troubling him. I answered every question he asked and presented my evidence to the best of my ability.

When we walked out of the jury room, Larry walked away from me and didn't say a word.

"Shit," I thought "this man has just hammered me for six straight hours. He performed one of the best jobs of prosecution I had ever witnessed. It was evident the note would be Melissa's biggest problem."

I walked into Larry's office and told him, "Good Job!" He looked up at me from his desk and said, "What's so damn good about it? Those poor kids are going to be indicted for first degree murder!"

"Damn Larry, I thought that's what you wanted!" I said.

I could see he was more upset than I was and he still had to interview at least four or five more people.

The Grand Jury deliberated for hours and hours, but finally reached a verdict.

They issued a True Bill for the charge of First Degree Murder. If charged as adults they could receive the death penalty at the very least life in prison.

You know? I did my job, we all did, but this case, my God, it was emotionally draining. These two kids were sweet and respectful. They were polite and courteous to everyone they came in contact with.

The public defender and the state attorney's office began some intense negotiations after the indictment. The kids were on pins and needles. We were all a little nervous. I spoke with Amanda and Robert and they were still convinced that they had done the right thing. Robert said he would do it again and had absolutely no remorse.

A plea agreement was finally reached between the state attorney and the public defender. The agreement was presented to the judge who accepted it.

It was finally over. Amanda and Robert were both sentenced to supervised probation with a multitude of stipulations. Each would serve until aged twenty-five.

Cooler heads did prevail in this case. Thank God.

But I don't think it ever really will be over. The stains of agony and pain are indelibly embossed on these two children's past and future. The investigators on this case walked away with a different perspective on life and I am sure treated their children with just a little more love and compassion than previously.

"Robert! Robert! Wake up son!" Robert opened his eyes, but refused to look in the direction where the words were coming from. He started breathing heavily and trembling as he lay in his bed. His body was covered with goose bumps. He swallowed hard, then cleared his throat and lifted his head from the pillow. "Tom?" he asked. "Wha …," Then a deep sigh and "wha …" again. He couldn't get the words out. He was paralyzed with fear. He finally looked into the corner of the room and saw Tom standing there, bleeding from his chest.

"Finish it Robert. Kill your mother! Kill your damn mother, Robert!" Tom screamed. Robert gasped for air and jumped out of the bed. He looked back into the corner and Tom was gone. Sweat was dripping from his forehead.

"It was just a dream. It was just a dream!" His wife told him, hugging him in a protective embrace. "It's okay, baby," she said as Robert lay back down to sleep. "That was a long time ago, honey!" she said, as she attempted to comfort Robert.

Robert experienced these awful nightmares for several years after the shooting, but they subsided with time and he was able to go on with his life. As of today, Robert has become a productive member of society. He moved back to Tennessee, got married and had children of his own.

As of the date of this book the only two times Robert has ever resorted to violence was when he killed that poor little squirrel in Tennessee with his BB gun and when he unloaded a 38-caliber pistol into his stepfather.

He said he still regrets killing that squirrel.

Amanda also got married and moved back to Tennessee where she, too, had children of her own. By the grace of God she was able to overcome her past and move on with her life.

Melissa made a 180-degree turn in her life. She married a State Trooper and remained in Central Florida where they still live today.

As for me? Well, I left law enforcement in 1993 and followed a career in marketing and sales. It's been a long time since this case, but it's as clear in my mind today as it was then.

Made in the USA
Lexington, KY
20 September 2015